FIGHTING MACHINES

by Bill Gunston OBE FRAES, John Guy,
Iain MacKenzie and Commander Jeff Tall OBE RN

ticktock

MUSTANG PILOT

In the Second World War one of the best Allied fighter planes was the North American P-51 Mustang. The pilots' helmets were fitted headphones, and on the front they carried an oxygen mask and integral microphone.

Copyright © 2006 *ticktock* Entertainment Ltd. First published in Great Britain by ticktock Media Ltd.,
Unit 2, Orchard Business Centre, North Farm Road, Tunbridge Wells, Kent TN2 3XF, Great Britain.

A CIP catalogue record for this book is available from the British Library.
ISBN 1 86007 571 1
Printed in China.

Picture Credits: t=top, b=bottom, c=centre, l=left, r=right.
AFP/Corbis-Bettman: 82l. AKG Photo London: 6cb, 6-7cb, 7cr, 7t, 8bl, 8-9c, 9c, 9br, 10br, 13cr, 14tl, 16-17c, 16l, 20tl, 21bl, 21tl, 25tl, 28-29, 45l, 55b, 64bl, 65tr, 72br, 72bl, 75tl, 95br, 94c, 82bl, 83br, 83tl. Ancient Art & Architecture: 7br, 10tl, 10-11c, 11tr, 13tl, 13br, 14bl, 18bl, 18tl, 18c, 18-19c, 21tr, 22-23cb. Ann Ronan @ Image Select: 10bl, 11br, 12-13c, 12-13cb, 13tr, 19br, 20bl, 20br, 22bl, 23tr, 24br, 24bl, 26cl, 26bl, 26-27cb, 27tr, 27tl, 28c, 37b, 38tr, 39tr, 41tl, 42c, 42cb, 44tl, 50tl, 50bl. Aviation Photographs International: 51bl, 51br, 54tl, 55t, 56b, 57c, 63tr, 72tl, 75c, 76-77b, 78-79t, 79tc, 90tl, 90bl, 90-91c, 91tr, 92b, 93t, 102b, 104cl, 104tl, 104-105c, 106l. Bridgeman: 15br, 17l, 17br. British Library: 17tr, 33tl. Bundesarchiv: 76-77c. Chris Fairclough/Image Select: 24tl, 26tl. Colorific: 105tr. Corbis-Bettman: 12l, 25r, 83br, 94br. The Defence Picture Library: 97tr, 98tl. et archive: 28tr, 28tl, 59tr. Fine Art Photographic Library: 25c. Frank Spooner Pictures: 96-97cb, 98-99, 99c. FPG International: 74tl, 75b, 104bl, 106tl. Giraudon (Paris): 10-11cb, 15bl, 21br, 30tl, 46tl, 46bl, 47t, 47br (x 2). Hulton Deutch: 73tr, 73b, 74b, 79br, 81bl. Hulton Getty: 24b, 52tl, 65b. Image Select: 6tl, 6-7ct, 8tl, 9tr, 19tr, 23br, 27br, 39br, 45tr, 46br, 47t, 51tl, 64tl, 65l, 78bl, 83c, 82-83cb. Jim Sugar Photography/Corbis: 89br. Kobal Collection: 107tr. Kozlowski Productions: 81tr. Lawson Wood/Corbis: 101tr. Mary Evans Picture Library: 22-23ct, 51tr, 53tr, 53cr, 55cr, 56-57t, 62t, 63br, Martin Baker: 80-81c. The Military Picture Library: 96b, 96l. National Maritime Museum: 15tr, 16tl, 30bl, 30-31c, 31t, 31b, 32br, 32tl, 32bl, 32-33c, 33br, 34tl, 34bl, 34-35c, 35tr, 35cr, 35b, 36tl, 36bl, 36r, 37tr, 37c, 37tl, 38tl, 38bl, 38-39c, 43br, 58tl, 59tl. Philip Jarrett: 54-55, 56tl, 62bl, 62br, 62-63c, 75tr, 76tl, 76bl, 77tr, 78-79b, 92tr, 103tr, 103b, 107bl. Pix: 8bl, 100bl. Quadrant Picture Library: 53b, 57t, 78tl, 80tl, 95tr, 102tl, 106r. Rex Features London: 82-83ct, 94r, 94tl. Royal Navy Submarine Museum: 40tl, 40bl, 41cb, 41tl, 42tl, 43r, 44-45c, 45tl, 45br, 45tr, 48-49c, 49cl, 60tl, 60cb, 61br, 66tl, 66bl, 67tl, 68tl, 68l, 68tr, 86tl, 86c, 87bl, 87tl, 70l, 71b, 84-85, 85tl, 88tl. Salamander Picture Library: 52-53b, 57b, 72c, 80-81c, 91bl, 92-93c, 105bl, 106bl. Sipa Press (Paris): 95l. UPI/Corbis-Bettmann: 67c. US Department of Defense/Corbis: 84tl, 100r. US Navy: 97br. Vosper Thornycroft (UK) Ltd: 99tl. Yefim Gordon: 103r. Yogi inc/Corbis: 85tr, 87tr, 89c, 89tr, 100tr, 100c, 101b.

CONTENTS

INTRODUCTION

Ever since man first appeared on Earth there have been conflicts. At first, squabbles were settled with fists, but as technology advanced, people began to fight with weapons. Combat moved from the land to the sea, and eventually even the skies became a battlefield. No other species has devoted such energy to harming other members.

HISTORY OF WARFARE

The way in which war has been fought has changed dramatically over the ages. At first battles were fought between individuals, then small groups, before eventually the first armies were formed. The battle arenas themselves have also changed. By the 7th-8th centuries, combat moved to fortified buildings such as castles but by the medieval era, tactics had begun to change. Armies had started to confront each other in open fields. Mounted on horses, they would attack each other with slashing swords and other blades. Finally, the 20th century saw the arrival of the first global wars. Between 1914-1918, World War I claimed the lives of over five million people, while between 1939-1945, a further four million men and women lost their lives in World War II. This book provides the background to the complete history of warfare.

SCIENCE & TECHNOLOGY

The first weapons were made around five thousand years ago with the manufacturing of spears and knives. Made from stone, then metal, they were crude instruments but were capable of causing horrific damage. These weapons gradually became more sophisticated with the introduction of materials such as bronze and iron. Great civilisations such as the Romans used these metals to make increasingly more vicious weapons and also to make body armour to protect themselves from injury. The book goes on to chart dramatic moments such as the invention of the gun, right up to the present day with the awesome destructive power of the hydrogen bomb and the damage this terrible weapon is capable of causing.

LAND, SEA & SKY

The book looks at the development of combat on land, sea and air. It details the first sea battles in the 13th century, and the invention of the first submarines in the 18th and 19th centuries. The book ends with developments in the 20th century, when combat took to the skies for the first time just a few years after the Wright brothers' first flight, and huge tanks rumbled across enemies lines causing terrible damage. It looks at the use of sophisticated satellite technology, and recent developments such as tracking devices.

GREAT LEADERS

The book also looks at the role of individuals in warfare. It details the history of great war leaders and the roles they have played in motivating their forces, from Julius Caesar and Bodeacia to modern figures such as Mao Tse-Tung, Sir Winston Churchill, General Patton and Norman Schwarzkopf. Find out about the tactics of these great war leaders and their triumphs and mistakes.

LATEST DEVELOPMENTS

Despite the tragedy of two world wars and the end of the Cold War, countries still continue to plough huge amounts of money into protecting themselves from aggressors. Read on to take an in-depth look at the latest developments in the world of the military, from infra-red technology to the most destructive nuclear weaponry. You can also learn about the most recent conflicts and speculate over future developments in a continually turbulent world.

Inspirational Leaders of the Past

Throughout history there have been a handful of leaders whose deeds and exploits set them apart from all others. Most were military generals who led their armies in the conquest of other lands. Included among these are Alexander the Great, who extended the Greek empire in the twilight years of that civilisation in the 4th century BC and laid the ground for the Roman empire that followed. Rulers such as Alexander and Julius Caesar were intent not just upon conquest but also on the spread of their civilisations. By contrast, the ruthless Mongolian leader Genghis Khan desired only power and exploitation. Other great leaders arose in trying to defend their homelands from invasion, as with Hannibal, the brilliant Carthaginian general, and Boudicca, the Celtic British queen, both of whom tried to halt the advances of the Roman empire.

ALEXANDER THE GREAT (356-323 BC)

Alexander the Great inherited his father's kingdom of Macedonia when just 20 years old. An inspired leader, he always led his army from the front of the battlefield. By 323 BC, when he died prematurely of fever, he had extended his rule, and the Greek empire, to Persia (now Iran), Egypt, Asia Minor and India.

GENGHIS KHAN (c.1162-1227)

In the 13th century, the Mongols established one of the largest empires ever known, extending over most of China, southern Russia, much of eastern Europe and Asia Minor (what we now term the Middle East). The empire was centred on Mongolia and its most powerful and ruthless ruler was Genghis Khan. He was a cruel man whose name roughly translates to 'ruler of all men'. He is believed to have been responsible for over 30 million deaths.

GEORGE WASHINGTON (1732-99)

George Washington was born in Virginia and fought for the English in the French and Indian wars of 1754-63. An honest man of humble birth, his integrity is said to have inspired his fellow Americans. He spoke out against British rule and led the revolution for independence, becoming the first President of the newly-founded United States of America in 1787.

HANNIBAL (247-182 BC)

Rome's second attempt to invade Carthage, a city-state in North Africa, was thwarted by Hannibal (a brilliant young Carthaginian general) in the Second Punic War (218-202 BC). He marched his army, together with 40 African war elephants, around North Africa, crossed to Spain and then proceeded to cross the Alps into Italy and strike Rome from the north, where it least expected attack. He defeated the Romans at Cannae in 216 BC, but was eventually beaten in 202 BC.

THE DUKE OF WELLINGTON (1769-1852)

Arthur Wellesley, 1st Duke of Wellington, was of Irish birth and began his distinguished career as a soldier. He quickly rose through the ranks, but is best remembered for defeating Napoleon Bonaparte at Waterloo in 1815. He returned home a hero and entered politics, becoming Prime Minister in 1828. He was the first leader also to be Commander-in-Chief of the British Army since Cromwell.

NAPOLEON I (1769-1821)

Napoleon Bonaparte was a French ruler and military leader of rare military genius with ideals of world domination, who is said to have inspired Hitler. War broke out between Britain and France in 1793 and resumed again in 1803, after a short truce. Napoleon won resounding victories in Italy (1796), Belgium (1797), Austria (1805), Prussia (1806) and Russia (1807). A charismatic man, he inspired his troops by looking after their well-being and ensuring they were well-fed. He was eventually defeated by a combined allied army and spent the remainder of his life in exile.

JULIUS CAESAR (c.100-44 BC)

Julius Caesar began his career in the Roman army and quickly rose to the rank of general. He also became a leading statesman in the Roman Senate. He conquered Gaul and invaded Britain (in 55 and 54BC). He was later ordered by the senate to disband the army but invaded Italy instead. Rome had been a republic, ruled by elected statesmen, but Caesar became power-hungry and wanted to rule alone, as emperor. He became dictator from 49 BC on. It was feared that he was becoming too powerful which led to his assassination on 15th March 44 BC by his fellow politicians. He was deified after his death, later Roman emperors assuming the godhead and title Caesar in his honour.

Inspirational Leaders of the 20th Century

MAO TSE-TUNG (1893-1976)

Mao Tse-Tung was a revolutionary Chinese leader and founder of the Chinese Communist Party (1921). When the Communists broke from the Chinese Nationalists in 1927, civil war broke out. He inspired an almost fanatical zeal among his followers and initiated a cultural revolution, making promises of social equality. He was Chairman of the Chinese Communist Party between 1949-76.

Whereas many of the inspirational leaders of the past have led their country to victory during campaigns of aggression, many of the greatest leaders of modern times have come to prominence more for their inspired resistance to aggressors, answering their nation's call during its hour of greatest need. A notable exception, perhaps, was Adolf Hitler (1889-1945) who certainly received fanatical devotion from his followers. However, the scale of atrocities during World War II prevents us from calling him an 'inspired' leader when the memories and consequences of that conflict are still too close in time to judge objectively. Future historians, with the benefit of the longer view, may judge him differently.

EISENHOWER (1890-1969)

Dwight David Eisenhower ('Ike') was a distinguished general in World War II, who afterwards went on to become the 34th U.S. President in 1952. He was the Supreme Commander of the Allied Forces in the 1944 invasion of Europe and also of NATO. forces in Europe after the war. He developed a personal approach to leadership that made him seem less remote to his troops.

SIR WINSTON CHURCHILL (1874-1965)

Considered by many to be one of the world's greatest wartime leaders, Winston Churchill (shown far left) succeeded in uniting the people of Britain and boosting morale when all seemed lost during the early years of World War II. A great orator, his rousing radio speeches lifted the spirits of an all but defeated nation. He became a Conservative M.P. in 1900, joined the Liberals in 1904 and reverted to the Tories in 1929. He became Prime Minister of a coalition government in Britain during the Second World War. In 1963 he was granted honorary US citizenship.

GANDHI (1869-1948)

Not all great leaders came from a military background. Some like Mohandas Karamchand ('Mahatma') Gandhi, preferred a more peaceful resolution to human rights problems. An Indian nationalist leader, Gandhi spent 21 years campaigning for equal rights for Indians in South Africa. He advocated a policy of non-violent civil disobedience against British rule in India which, from a military perspective, was difficult to contain. He was a leading figure in securing India's eventual independence in 1947.

NELSON MANDELA (b.1918)

Nelson Mandela joined the African National Congress in 1944, so beginning his career as a black nationalist leader. He campaigned avidly for a free, multi-racial and democratic society in South Africa. Imprisoned between 1964-90 he became a political martyr, continuing to inspire the cause from his prison cell. He was eventually released following world-wide opposition to his imprisonment and was elected the first black president of South Africa in 1994.

'STORMING NORMAN'

The U.S. General Norman Schwarzkopf (nicknamed 'Storming Norman') led the allied attack on Iraq in the Gulf War of 1990-91. In August 1990 Saddam Hussein, dictator of Iraq, invaded neighbouring Kuwait when talks about oil quotas broke down. The United Nations imposed sanctions on Iraq followed by a short high-tech war, which was all over by April 1991. Schwarzkopf's raid on Iraq, in the final stages of the war, is said to have been inspired by Hannibal's attack on Rome.

GENERAL PATTON (1885-1945)

Like other great U.S. leaders, General George Smith Patton believed that personal contact with his troops was essential for good morale. His most noteworthy campaign was in 1944-45, when he led the 7th Army across France and Germany following the D-Day landings.

Early Weapons & Warfare

The need for fortification has been with us since humans have been on the planet. Initially, strong dwellings were needed only as protection against the elements or from wild animals, but as man became more civilised, and hence more territorial, so the need grew to protect himself against his fellow man. That need has been with us ever since and seems likely to remain so. In the same way the primitive weapons that had been devised purely for hunting came to have a dual purpose: they began to be used to injure and kill *people*. The ingenuity with which humans have devoted their skills to destroying their own kind is perhaps a sad reflection on our species. No other animal expends such energy in pursuit of killing.

BRONZE AGE SHIELDS

Tribal leaders in Bronze Age Europe (c.2000BC-c.600BC) decorated both their weapons and their armour to display their position in the community. This magnificent bronze shield dates from the 1st century AD and was discovered at Battersea, in London, preserved in the mud of the River Thames. Made from bronze and gold, and decorated with red glass studs (then a valuable material), the raised patterns were fashioned by hammering from the reverse side.

THE AGE OF METAL

Prior to c. 2500 BC most tools and weapons were fashioned from stone. Hammers and maces were made by simply lashing a shaped stone to a wooden handle, while sharp flints, shaped to a point, made ideal spear and arrow heads. At about that time, however, the technique of manufacturing metals from natural ores developed. This hard-edged, bronze dagger (made from pouring liquid tin and copper into a mould) revolutionised weapon design.

THE MACE

Along with the spear, the mace is one of the earliest weapons used by man. In prehistoric times clubs were probably fashioned from the thigh bones of animals, or from hard, knobbly wood. The mace is a direct derivative of the simple club. By medieval times it had been fashioned into a formidable weapon, with the rounded end made of flanged metal and often reinforced with studs or spikes to pierce metal armour and inflict horrific injuries.

HILLFORTS

From about 1000 BC a type of fortification known as hillforts began to appear in Britain. They remained in use throughout the Iron Age until the Roman occupation. They were large communal, defensive enclosures, more akin perhaps to townships than individual fortifications. They consisted usually of a large, levelled enclosure on top of a hill, surrounded by one or more massive earthen ramparts, usually surmounted by timber palisades or stone walls.

BROCHS & DUNS

From about 200 BC another type of fortification, known as brochs and duns, began to appear in Iron Age Britain, principally in Scotland. They were hollow stone towers, about 40-50ft. high, usually circular or D-shaped, with timber buildings arranged around a central courtyard. Unlike hillforts, which were communal defences, these towers were the fortified farmhouses of a single family or small group of people. The impressive example shown here is at Furness, in the Orkney Isles.

THE ORIENT

In the West, an important purpose of armour (other than to offer its wearer protection) was to impress onlookers with its finery and craftsmanship. By contrast, the primary objective of this horrific Japanese mask was to intimidate and terrify the enemy – an early form of psychological warfare.

THE BIBLE AS HISTORY

This picture shows Joshua (chosen by Moses to lead the Israelites) defeating the Ammonites at Jericho. It is typical of many Biblical stories, which can be viewed as a collection of early historical writings, giving valuable insights into pre-Christian society in the Middle East.

Warfare in the Ancient World

Although man has probably always made weapons and waged war against his fellow man, it was the introduction of metal that revolutionised warfare. Swords were not very effective when only flint was available for making a blade – the weapon would have been too fragile and too heavy. The first swords were made of copper but were too soft and could not hold an edge. They became more effective after the introduction of tin (about 2500 BC) to make bronze, a hard metal which retained its cutting edge and was relatively easy to make. Although the Bronze Age is commonly held to have given way to the Iron Age at about 600 BC, in reality there was considerable overlap. Bronze was manufactured for weapons well into the Iron Age and iron was smelted as early as c.3000 BC in Asia Minor. Iron only gradually superseded bronze as the favourite material of warfare.

THE ROMANS

The emergence of Rome as the dominant city-state in the classical world owed much to the ancient Greeks and the Etruscans, who came from Asia Minor (or perhaps the Orient), establishing a number of self-governing city-states in Italy. The Romans quickly established a well-trained and well-equipped army that became the most efficient military force then known. A typical Roman legionnaire was equipped with a helmet, an oblong shield, a short sword and breastplate armour comprised of overlapping metal plates laced together, a type favoured by oriental armourers.

THE GREEKS

The ancient Greek army was largely a civilian force, each soldier supplying his own equipment so that the richest civilians became the best-equipped and most powerful soldiers. A typical soldier (known as a hoplite) was equipped with a bronze helmet (such as this bronze Corinthian example shown left, of c.500 BC) and a circular shield. Some soldiers carried short, bronze swords, but the usual weapon was a spear. The favoured method of attack was a massed assault by spearsmen to push an enemy back.

CHARIOTS

Horse-drawn chariots seem to have originated in the Near East, in Canaan, about 3000 BC. When the Egyptians extended their empire north, into Asia Minor, they brought back chariots and developed them into fast, light-weight fighting platforms. Chariots usually carried two men (one to control the horses and one to fight) and were employed throughout the ancient world. The example shown here comes from Babylon.

THE SIEGE OF TROY

In about 1184 BC Helen, wife of Menelaus, King of Sparta, was captured by the Trojans (Troy was a city-state in what is now part of Turkey). Menelaus's brother, Agamemnon, King of Mycenae, united the Greeks and attacked the city of Troy, but after 10 years was unable to capture it. The Greeks built a huge wooden horse, supposedly as a gift to the Trojans, and departed. Soldiers, hidden inside the horse, secretly opened the city gates to let in the returning Greek army, who then destroyed the city.

'GREEK FIRE'

'Greek Fire' was an early form of incendiary device employed by the ancient Greeks and remained in use, in differing forms, until medieval times. It is made from a compound of naphtha, saltpetre and sulphur, contained within earthenware pots, which were then set on fire and hurled at the enemy by the use of catapults. Because of the ingredients used, the flames would burn in water and so became a favourite weapon to use against an enemy's ships.

THE HITTITES

The Hittites (or 'sons of Heth') were a war-like people who occupied a large territory in what is now part of modern-day eastern Turkey. Their lands bordered the Mitanni (now part of Arabia) and Egypt. The Hittites were the first people to smelt iron extensively (from about 3000 BC) and their use of strong iron swords was probably instrumental in extending their empire over much of the Middle East.

Ancient Warships

Our information about the warships of the Ancient World comes from the frescoes of Minoan Crete, the carvings of Egypt and from the art and chronicles of Classical Greece and Rome. The Minoans had a navy by 1600 BC, probably the first in the world. Piracy is as old as human history and the Minoans wanted to protect their trading vessels - and to raid other ships! The ancient galley reached a peak in the Greek trireme. In this formidable vessel, with its three layers of oarsmen, the Greeks withstood the Persians at Salamis in 480 BC. Recent scholarship and marine archaeology have improved our understanding of ancient naval technology and warfare, enabling the reconstruction of an Athenian trireme. The Romans are not noted for their seamanship, but they defeated Carthage at sea and made the Mediterranean theirs. Rome only contested it again in civil war. The oar-driven galley remained a feature of the 'middle sea' for over 3,000 years.

THE FIRST SEA BATTLE?

This temple relief marks Pharaoh Rameses III's naval victory over the 'Sea Peoples' in 1176 BC. Tactics of the day were to grapple an opponent's rigging and try to capsize him, or to board and fight hand-to-hand. These Bronze Age ships were to lightly built to risk ramming an enemy.

The main weapon of the Greek ships was the heavy bronze ram. Mounted low on the bows, it could punch a hole clean through an enemy's hull.

OLYMPIAS REBORN

1987 saw the birth of the Athenian trireme, the classic warship of the Ancient Greeks. Reconstructed from evidence, this modern replica is formally a ship of the Hellenic Navy. With 170 oarsmen on three levels, she glides along at up to 9 knots. Unlike most galley oarsmen, the crews of the Ancient Greek city-states were made up of free men.

GREEK BIREME

Sails powered the galleys of the Ancient World on the open sea; the skilled oarsmen saved their strength for the attack - they were much more reliable than the wind when manoeuvring in a tight spot.

BATTLE OF ACTIUM

In 31BC a Roman fleet under Octavian wiped out Cleopatra's navy off the coast of Greece. Realising she was fighting a losing battle, the Egyptian queen and her consort, Mark Antony, slipped away to Alexandria and left the rest of the fleet to its fate. More than 400 ships were involved in the battle, imaginatively reconstructed in this 17th-century painting.

SWORD TO SWORD

Like the Greek warships, Roman galleys had rams, but the Roman soldiers were used to combat on land and preferred to use the spear and the sword. They usually fitted their warships with a hinged boarding plank (the *corvus*) which spiked into an enemy's deck and allowed

the soldiers to board the enemy ship and fight hand-to-hand. These small galleys, from a painting excavated at Pompeii, lack the corvus, but the heavily-armed marines are clearly visible.

TOWN SEAL

In time of war, a medieval ruler would demand ships from every port in his kingdom to swell his fleet. The seals and arms of many coastal towns show ships fitted with 'castles', in the bow and stern. These temporary fortified platforms gave some protection to the ship's archers and men-at-arms in battle.

Warships in the Dark Ages

Europe's 'Dark Ages', the centuries after the fall of Rome, left little historical record of warship development. However, many Viking warriors were buried on land in their boats and archaeological discoveries have provided much information about the boats of northern Europe and the restless peoples who built them. The 'Norsemen' were experienced sailors. In their longships they explored, raided and colonised. The descendants of these vessels are still used today, for fishing around the continent's northern and western fringe.

VIKING ATTACK!

The collapse of the western Roman Empire around AD 455 threw Europe into turmoil for centuries. The shores of the Baltic, the North Sea and beyond saw several seaborne invasions as restless peoples, such as the Vikings, sought new places to settle. The most fearsome feature of these raiding ships was the fighting prowess and single-minded violence of their crews.

THE VERSATILE VIKING SHIP

Vikings ravaged the coasts and rivers of Northern Europe, from Ireland to Russia. With 'clinker-built' hulls of overlapping planks, these ships were seaworthy enough to cross the Atlantic. The Vikings established colonies in Greenland and North America (which they called 'Vinland'). The longships' shallow draught (how low they sat in the water) allowed them upriver to explore inland.

THE TERRIBLE DRAGON

Until recent times, warships were often highly decorated. The Vikings favoured a frightening beast on the prow, to terrify the enemy. The dragon head, or *drakkar*, gave its name to the largest type of Norse warship. The Ancient Greeks painted an 'warlike glaring eye' above the ram on their ships, Spanish galleons were richly painted and gilded, and 18th-century ships-of-the-line had carved figureheads of heraldic figures. Even German submarines of World War II had insignia on their conning towers.

THE COG

Cogs were North European trading ships, but, like other types of the period, they could easily be adapted for war. The addition of fighting platforms fore and aft, and later a fighting platform at the masthead, would be enough to make this a warship.

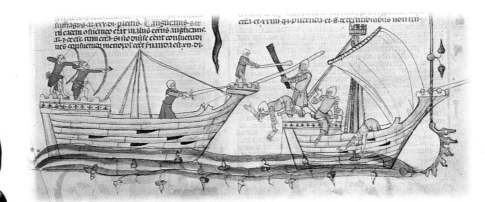

PIRATES AHOY!

Large-scale sea battles were relatively rare in the early Middle Ages but pirates were not! The tactics of fighting at sea were dictated by the weapons available - the bow, the spear, the broadsword and the battle axe. Fighting from a greater height gave a crucial advantage and so the temporary 'castles' soon became a permanent part of the ship's structure. Another medieval innovation came with the development of the stern rudder, which was a great advance on the steering oar.

SEA-GOING FORTRESS

From a 15th-century manuscript, this imaginary vessel shows a medieval landsman's notion of an ideal warship: a wooden castle garrisoned with armoured men-at-arms and propelled by oars rather than sails.

ARMOURED KNIGHTS

Throughout Europe the development of arms and armour followed much the same pattern and flourished with the development of the feudal system. As the feudal system of government subsided, so the methods of warfare changed and the need for armour declined. In the 11th century, armour consisted principally of a helmet and chain-mail tunic, made up of inter-connecting metal rings. Because knights (and all soldiers) were expected to supply their own weapons and armour as part of their feudal service, the more wealthy could afford elaborate suits of plate armour, as shown here. Armour became so heavy and ponderous by the end of the medieval period that it hampered fighting and gradually came to be used more for ceremonial occasions than in war.

TACTICAL SUPREMACY

Towards the end of the medieval period (from about the mid-14th century on) the tactics of warfare began to change. The emphasis shifted away from attacking and defending castles, once considered the most important of strategies, to open warfare in the field. By this time armies consisted mostly of paid soldiers and mercenaries rather that the untrained soldiers provided by the feudal system. At the Battle of Agincourt in 1415, during the 100 years' war with France, England won a resounding victory against the superior forces of France, by the tactical use of archers.

JAVANESE KRIS

This highly ornate sword, with its wavy blade, comes from Java and is typical of many Indonesian and south-east Asian swords. Known as a 'kris' its use was mainly ceremonial, though it was also used in combat. Decorated with gold, silver and ivory, the blade was usually made of iron, which was then treated with acid to create decorative patterns.

CHIVALRIC CODE

Its very strict chivalric code belied the often barbaric nature of medieval warfare. Battles would often be decided by negotiation rather than by fighting, or champions might be called upon to decide the outcome, each side selecting a single combatant, or group of knights, to fight on its behalf. If captured, knights were not usually killed, but held to ransom. Never the less injuries inflicted on the battle field were quite horrific, many dying from secondary infections rather than their wounds.

18

Medieval Weapons & Warfare

The period in history known as the Middle Ages, or medieval period, was for many parts of the world an era of great upheaval. In Europe particularly, great power struggles were waged between lords and kings in their thirst for land. Many of today's political boundaries were established in this time. Europe and Asia were dominated by the feudal system, or variations on it, in which kings ultimately owned all the land in their kingdom, which they let out to various lords. They in turn let out their land to sub-tenants, lesser barons or knights. The result was a virtually continuous struggle for power and supremacy between either the king and his barons, or between the barons as they jostled for position.

JAPANESE ARMOUR

The development of oriental arms and armour followed a completely different course from that in the West (or Occident). Japanese armour was intended to terrify and intimidate the enemy as much as to protect its wearer. The favoured form was a type known as scale armour, made by lacing together overlapping metal or leather plates, often lacquered. Helmets were fitted with wide, splayed neck guards.

LONGBOWS & CROSSBOWS

Although the longbow was the favoured weapon of attack in battle because it had a longer range and was faster to fire than the crossbow, the latter was favoured by castle defenders because it was more deadly at close range. The crossbow had to be pulled back (usually by a winding mechanism) and fired a bolt (about 1ft. long). Both weapons were preferred to early guns, which were dangerous and unreliable.

THE VIKINGS

Contrary to popular belief, the Vikings did not usually wear horned helmets, though some leaders may have worn them on ceremonial occasions. A typical Viking warrior wore a helmet, sometimes with terrifying face mask (such as the one shown here), a tunic of chain-mail (or leather) and a circular shield. His favourite weapons were an iron sword, battle axe, long spear or bow.

A longbow

A crossbow

An early Medieval cannon

Attack & Defence

THE GREAT WALL OF CHINA

The Great Wall of China is the only man-made feature on Earth that can be seen from outer space. It was ordered to be built by Emperor Shih Huang Ti in c.214 BC to keep out the Mongolian Huns to the north of China. Maintained and rebuilt several times since then, most of this massive construction, which runs for 2400 km/1500 miles, dates from the 15th - 16th centuries AD.

The twin principles of attack and defence have always gone hand-in-hand. Every advance in new methods of attack was met by a corresponding advance in defensive techniques. History demonstrates this pendulum swing throughout the ages, where first one side gained the advantage only to be almost immediately outmanoeuvred by the other. Nowhere is this better illustrated than in medieval siege warfare, as the series of illustrations on these two pages show. While no expense was spared in the development of new military technology and weaponry, defences became ever-more impregnable. The ingenuity of the human mind seems somehow to excel when faced with the problems of attack and counter attack, perhaps inspired by the basic instinct of survival. Many of the most significant advances in science and technology first began as part of a military strategy. The most spectacular example of this in the modern world, perhaps, is the development of the rocket, from the 'flying bombs' made by German scientists during World War II.

SIEGE TOWERS

There were many ways in which a fortress might be attacked. Archers could fire at defenders on the walls from behind wooden screens to give covering fire while others attempted to gain entry by scaling ladders or from the protection of a belfry. A belfry was a wooden tower that could be wheeled into position against the wall and then a drawbridge lowered from its top stage onto the wall top giving attackers direct access to the walls. However, ladders could be easily pushed away and belfries were susceptible to fire.

SIEGE ENGINES

There were a number of different siege engines to help attackers gain entry to a fortress, some so powerful that they remained in use long after the advent of guns. The mangonel (left) was a huge stone-throwing machine, similar to a catapult. Others were the ballista, a kind of giant crossbow, and the trebuchet, which resembled an enormous sling.

DEFENDING THE WALLS

Despite their bristling array of walls, towers and other defences, most castles were seldom called upon to withstand a siege. Their very presence acted as a deterrent and the outcome of confrontations was often decided by negotiation rather than by force. Sieges could last anything up to a year (or, exceptionally, longer) but were very costly. Most defenders surrendered when faced with disease or starvation.

JAPANESE CASTLES

Castles built in Japan and other oriental countries resemble, to western eyes, huge houses or temples and show few outward signs of being defensible. They were much stronger than they might first appear, however, with the living apartments ranged in tiers above a massive, featureless stone plinth that gave an attacker few opportunities to gain access. This view shows the 16th century Hiniesu Castle in Japan (Castle of the White Heron).

AGE-OLD METHODS

Methods of siege warfare changed little over the centuries and most of the siege engines described here were used by the Romans and even the ancient Greeks. Often the defenders inside a fortress also had their own siege engines to shower the attackers with stones or burning straw. They fired a variety of missiles, including stones, burning faggots, shrapnel or even dead horses to induce disease. Trebuchets could hurl a boulder weighing several hundredweight a distance of some hundreds of yards and could reduce a wall to rubble with concentrated fire.

SHRAPNEL BOMBS

The Chinese, although credited with its invention, were slow to realise the potential of gunpowder. Until the 15th century they confined its use to scaring away the enemy with loud explosions. They did, however, develop exploding shrapnel bombs, which they hurled among the enemy using traditional siege engines.

The Invention of the Gun

Probably no other single event has had so profound an effect upon the practices of warfare, or indeed society, than the invention of gunpowder and the subsequent development of guns. Weapons and warfare changed very little for much of man's history, relying almost solely on sharp-edged hand weapons. The development of firearms a mere 600 years ago, however, changed all that with a subsequent and dramatic increase in loss of life sustained during armed conflicts. Although the Chinese have usually been credited with the invention of gunpowder, some doubt has now been cast on this. There are several other claimants, including India, Arabia and Greece. Certainly, its full potential was not recognised until European scientists invented the gun, probably in the late 13th century.

THE DEVELOPMENT OF HAND GUNS

Early guns were unreliable and accidents were common. If too much powder was introduced or flaws appeared in their metal barrels, the guns were likely to explode. Artillery was a new and inexact science. The foremost problem was how to ignite the powder without the need to carry a lighted touch-paper.

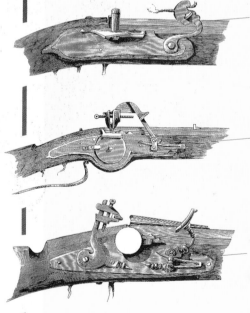

MATCHLOCKS: The earliest forms of hand-guns were matchlocks. They were fired by simply pouring the powder through a hole in the barrel and igniting it with a lighted touch-paper.
WHEEL-LOCKS: Wheel-locks dispensed with the need for lighting the gunpowder. A wheel mechanism created a spark by striking against iron pyrites in the chamber and so igniting the gunpowder.
FLINTLOCKS: In the flint-lock, the cock contained a piece of flint that, when triggered, hit against the metal hammer, creating a spark. By simultaneously exposing the gunpowder chamber, the powder was ignited.

THE FIRST GUNS

No-one knows who actually invented the gun. All that can be said with certainty is that the first illustration of a gun can be dated to 1326. No explanation is given so we must assume that guns were already commonplace and had been around for some years before that. Early guns were vase-shaped, but after about 1350 the more familiar hollow-tube shape made of wrought iron (shown here) began to appear, mounted on wooded supports. Projectiles were usually arrows or stone balls.

GUNPOWDER

It used to be claimed that the Chinese invented gunpowder (about 1045) but some doubt has now been cast on the accuracy of this date. What seems more likely is that several researchers in both Europe and Asia were working on similar formulae simultaneously. Either way, the full potential of gunpowder was not realised until the late 12th/early 13th centuries, when the first guns appeared. Its early use in China had been confined to making fireworks or creating large explosions to frighten an enemy (as seen here).

FRIAR BACON

Roger Bacon (c.1214-92) was an English Franciscan Friar who was in many ways ahead of his time. A scholar and scientist, he was very conscious of the superstitious times in which he lived and wrote down the results of his experiments in code to avoid persecution. Whether or not Friar Bacon was carrying out his own independent research or studying books brought back from China is not clear. What is certain is that he was the first person to write down the formula (c.1250) so that gunpowder could be manufactured to a consistent standard.

THE END OF AN ERA

Although the development of firearms has often been credited with sounding the death knell of the medieval castle, this was not the case. Early guns were neither reliable nor powerful enough to have much effect on stout castle walls. By the time guns were capable of causing substantial damage to stone walls, the day of the medieval castle had already passed.

A number of castles were either built, or altered, to accommodate guns, usually small handguns. The most common method was to change the more traditional cross-shaped arrow loop (shown here) to one resembling a key-hole shape. The gun barrel was passed through the circular hole while the gunner used the slot as a sighting line.

Warfare Since the Middle Ages

THE ENGLISH CIVIL WAR

The English Civil War of 1642-49 was fought between Royalists (known as Cavaliers) and Parliamentarians (the Roundheads) and was the result of many years of conflict between the monarchy and parliament in deciding who should rule the country. In February 1645 Parliament created a revolutionary new military system, the New Model Army. Nationally organised and trained, and regularly paid, it dispensed with the need for mercenaries.

Although we nowadays often adopt the somewhat complacent view that bloody warfare belongs to the Middle Ages, the truth is that, not only has mankind never been free of war, but by far the worst conflicts have occurred in modern times, particularly in terms of casualties. Casualties in wars used to be confined mostly to those involved in the actual fighting, because of the hand-to-hand nature of the weapons used. The development of firearms and, more particularly, impersonal weapons such as bombs, however, which can inflict harm upon an enemy across great distances, has meant that civilian casualties are now very much a part of modern warfare, whereas before they were comparatively rare. Although it might sound absurd, in the past there was a kind of code of war. Today it is very much more impersonal with death and destruction inflicted by remote control.

CHANGING STRATEGIES

Before the full potential of the discovery of gunpowder was realised, with the development of firearms, its explosive properties were used to good effect in blasting the walls and gates of fortifications.

AMERICAN CIVIL WAR

The American Civil War was fought between eleven southern states (the Confederates) and the northern (Union) states between 1861-65. The resulting conflict was a particularly bloody encounter. A scorched-earth policy by the Unionists resulted in many Confederate families being made homeless. Civilian and military prisoners were crammed into 'concentration camps', where many died of disease. Short of men, money and supplies, the Confederacy was eventually forced to surrender.

CHARGE OF THE LIGHT BRIGADE

The infamous 'Charge of the Light Brigade', which took place during the Crimean War, fought between Britain and Russia in 1854-56, was one of Britain's worst military disasters. Confused orders and incompetent officers resulted in a lightly armed cavalry charge straight towards the massed Russian guns. Strategists were forced to rethink their methods of attack as a result of such catastrophes.

SAMURAI WARRIORS

Samurai warriors were an elite caste of bodyguards employed by noblemen in medieval Japan. They followed a very strict code and treated their swords with an almost religious reverence. It was said that, once drawn, their swords, which were two-handed with slightly curved blades, could not be sheathed again until they had drawn blood. The Japanese martial art of Kendo uses the traditional swords and face masks once used by Samurai warriors.

AERIAL ATTACK

Airships were invented in 1900. Known as Zeppelins after their designer, Ferdinand Graf Zeppelin, they were huge, gas-filled dirigibles, but with a fuselage structure beneath the skin. They were cigar-shaped, with tail fins and an engine mounted in a cockpit suspended beneath, making them surprisingly manoeuvrable.

The Development of Firearms

BOAT POWER

Once it was understood how to make guns safe to use, people started to look for new ways to use gunpowder. The earliest torpedo boats were steam launches fitted with an explosive charge on a pole. This was run out over the bows and rammed against the target's hull. Although they sound dangerous, the charge exploded outward, and the small torpedo boats made a tricky target.

Following the initial discovery of gunpowder, it was some time before anyone had the idea of using the explosive power of the substance to propel an object and use it as a weapon of war. Early guns were fired by placing the powder and shot down the length of the barrel and ramming down hard. This method was known as muzzle loading. Accidents were common and the method was very time-consuming, particularly important when under fire in the heat of battle. It soon became obvious that it would be quicker and easier to load a gun from the breech, or firing end, but this would necessitate a second opening into the barrel that had somehow to be closed securely at the moment of fire to prevent mishaps.

BREECH-LOADING HANDGUNS

Although breech-loading cannon appeared probably as early as the 14th century, safe, breech-loading handguns were not successfully introduced until the early 18th century. The obvious dangers were the risk of burning or explosion in the face of the firer if the chamber was not properly sealed. The first breech-loading rifle appeared in 1812 but did not come into general service until 1848.

NEW LINES OF DEFENCE

The introduction of artillery had a profound effect upon the design of fortifications. To begin with guns were simply accommodated in medieval castles by adapting arrow loops for the purpose, but as guns became more reliable and powerful new types of defences had to be designed to accommodate the new, larger guns and to protect against the effects of cannon fire. Medieval castles, which were already in decline by the 15th century, presented too large a target for gunners. Forts built after about 1500 were low to the ground with massive earthen embankments behind the walls to lessen the impact of incoming fire. The old-style battlements were replaced with deeply splayed embrasures with circular or pointed bastions to deflect shot and give the guns maximum field of fire.

AUTOMATIC GUNS

The development of automatic guns became possible after the introduction of metal cartridges. The first machine gun, or rapid-firing gun, was patented by an American, Dr. Richard Gatling, in 1862. It employed several barrels that rotated in turn. In 1883 the design of machine guns was revolutionised by Hiram S. Maxim, another American. His single-barrelled gun utilised the recoil action, which was used to load, fire and eject simultaneously. The gun was cooled by a water jacket covering the barrel and was capable of firing up to 650 rounds a minute.

BOMBARDS

By the mid-15th century, gunmakers were beginning to perfect their art. They produced guns that were both more reliable and less likely to explode and also of a much larger size. They were usually cast in bronze or, more commonly, wrought iron, consisting of separate iron tubes, held together with iron hoops. The largest cannons were known as bombards and some reached huge proportions, up to 18ft. long (5.5m), 18tons/tonnes in weight with a calibre of 25ins. (63.5cm).

FIXED BAYONETS

Until the development of rapid firing and repeating guns, when an enemy approached too closely soldiers had to resort to old-fashioned hand-to-hand fighting. Often infantrymen, right up until the end of the 19th century, still carried swords and most had a bayonet, a kind of detachable spear-head, that could be fixed to the end of a rifle.

HOW THE WEST WAS WON

It has often been claimed that guns were responsible for white immigrants being able to over-run the native Americans. While this is undoubtedly true, it is only part of the story, for what really 'won the West' was the development of automatic weapons, capable of firing several rounds of ammunition without re-loading. The first hand-operated revolver appeared in 1818 and in 1836 Samuel Colt patented a percussion revolver with an automatically revolving chamber.

RULE *BRITANNIA*

The *Britannia* of 1682 was an early first-rate line-of-battle ship. The largest ships of their day, these impressive warships could carry over 100 guns on three decks and needed a crew of over 800 men. Ships like this were used for 200 years. The *Victory*, Lord Nelson's flagship at Trafalgar, is the only surviving ship of this type.

THE FIRST SEA BATTLE

Although ships had been a feature of many battles, the Battle of Sluys in 1340 is generally regarded as being the first truly naval battle. Edward III defeated the French navy during the 100 years' war and established English supremacy of the Channel. There is some evidence to suggest that guns were mounted on board some of the ships, making this the first use of firepower in a naval conflict.

UNDERWATER ATTACK

Prior to 1900, submarines were used mostly for reconnaissance work, but afterwards, once fitted with torpedo tubes, they became a very real threat to shipping. The electrically-powered *Holland*, shown here, was launched in 1897 and three years later was put into general service in the U.S. navy.

Battles at Sea Since the Middle Ages

The control of seaways has always been an essential part of warfare but, for the most part, ships were used to transport men, equipment and supplies, and not as fighting vessels. There is some evidence to suggest that the Greeks and Romans may have mounted siege engines such as ballistas, large catapult-like machines, to hurl missiles or fire upon an enemy, but mostly ships were used as simple fighting platforms for soldiers. Even up to the 16th century, when cannon were mounted on ships, the guns were used to disable a ship so that the soldiers could overrun the crew; ships were expensive to build and it was considered better to capture and repair an enemy ship rather than sink it.

BATTLE OF TRAFALGAR

Admiral Horatio, Lord Nelson (1758-1805) won a decisive naval victory against the French at Cape Trafalgar in 1805, establishing Britain as the foremost naval power in Europe. British warships at that time could fire a broadside every 90 seconds, twice as fast as any of their opponents.

Warships in the 15th~16th Centuries

L ittle is known about the great ships of the 15th and 16th centuries, despite the recovery of Henry VIII's fighting carrack, the *Mary Rose*, which capsized and sank off Portsmouth in 1545. This historic ship's construction suggests she had been rebuilt to carry heavier armament than when she was new, and may have been one of the first generation of ships to fire guns on the broadside. Ships like this resulted from an exchange of ideas and design features over generations of trade between Northern Europe and the Mediterranean. Southern shipbuilding techniques were applied to northern ships, while in the Mediterranean the northern square sail was adopted, creating the 'modern' three-masted ship, which was highly seaworthy and had a large capacity for cargo. The imposing features of the grandest carracks and galleons flattered the vanity of the late Renaissance rulers, and the ships became a byword for wealth and power.

'FÊTE DE LA FLOTTE PORTUGAISE'

Carracks were the chief carriers and protectors of trade for the Spanish and Portuguese and their New World colonies in the 1500s. Their importance was celebrated in ritual and in art, as in this illustration of a royal regatta in 1513. The richly-decorated galleys and barges of the dignitaries occupy the foreground, but their fortune had been made by the carracks in the background.

THE GALLEON

The galleon had finer lines and lower castles than the carrack, making her both faster and easier to handle. Not all galleons were warships, but they were often heavily armed. The type was popular with the Spanish bringing treasures back from the Americas. Long after the true galleon had disappeared, large and richly-laden Spanish ships were known as 'galleons'.

'PORTUGUESE CARRACKS OFF A ROCKY COAST'

The *Santa Caterina do Monte Sinai* was a Portuguese carrack of about 1520. She is shown here with the typically vast, billowing mainsail of a Mediterranean carrack. The carrack combined the design and rigging features of the northern cog with the frame-first shipbuilding tradition of the Mediterranean. Three-masted versions were known by the mid-1400s, and in the early 1500s the big carracks were armed with guns that fired through broadside gunports. These were the capital ships of their day.

SHIPS OF STATE

This scene shows Henry VIII on his way to meet Francis I, King of France in 1520. The painting was done later and in fact shows the three and four-masted carracks of around 1540. They are equipped with gunports in the hull, though at the time of Henry's visit guns were still mounted on the open decks and in the castles. A huge number of guns were carried by some ships: inventories from the 1490s show some with as many as 200.

OAR-SOME POWER

The galley was a common sight around the Mediterranean until the early 1800s. One feature that continued from ancient times was the use of condemned criminals or even slaves as oarsmen. The guns of this Venetian galley are mounted on a platform in the bows - the only place where these lightly-built ships were strong enough to support such heavy weaponry.

FLEETS OF FANCY

A first-rate 100-gun ship was built at Chatham, England in 1670, *Prince* was one of Charles II's 'Great Ships'. Rebuilt and renamed *Royal William* in 1692, she was broken up in 1714. The cost of carved decoration in major warships like this was so high that in 1704 the Admiralty issued orders to limit this fancy 'gingerbread work', as it was called.

THE STERN CABINS

Officers were quartered aft (towards the stern). Each had a private cabin – however small – and the Admiral and Captain had spacious accommodation. But the crew lived in cramped conditions: they had to sling their hammocks above the cannons.

THE POOP

The sails on the mizzen-mast were controlled and signal flags were hoisted from the poop, which was the highest deck.

PUNISHING PUMPS

Wooden ships leak. The bilges, in the bottom of the hull, had to be pumped out regularly. This back-breaking chore was often given to men as punishment for minor offences.

STEERING

The steering wheel was not invented until around 1700. Before then, a vertical pole on the inboard end of the tiller, the whipstaff, controlled the steering.

SHIP'S BONES

The massive oak timbers which made up the skeleton of the ship had to be well-seasoned. Part-completed ships were often left in the shipyard for years to 'season in frame'.

THE SHIP'S GUNS

During the 17th century, the biggest seagoing guns were 'cannons of seven' (42-pounders) and demi-cannons (32-pounders).

SAIL PLANS

The rig of ships evolved during the 1600s. There was much experimentation with sail plans but the versatile three-masted rig was adopted as standard in larger ships. Small craft preferred the single-masted gaff rig, developed in the Netherlands. Here a Dutch warship salutes a Dutch State yacht.

Warships in the 17th~18th Centuries

There was little peace in the 17th and early 18th centuries, and when the warring nations briefly ceased their religious and political conflicts, warships were kept busy stopping piracy and protecting the valuable and growing trade with new markets in the East. This was the age when line-of-battle tactics were developed: the 'Great Ships', the first and second-rates with three decks of guns, were built to fight in that line. Smaller ships, forerunners of frigates, scouted for the fleet, and specialist shore bombardment vessels first appeared. It was also the period when artists first began to make reliable portraits of ships in paintings and models.

THE 'BOMB'

The bomb vessel, invented by the French in the 1680s, carried one or two mortars that fired explosive shells. Built to withstand the shock of firing, this heavy vessel featured a two-masted ketch rig.

ANCHORS AWEIGH!

The only mechanical aids in tasks like raising the anchors or hoisting the sails on their yards were the capstains. They lessened the burden, but still needed strong men to turn them.

PAINTED SHIPS

This model of the English 80-gun third-rate ship *Boyne* of 1692, shows just how highly decorated ships became. Carved by the finest artists and craftsmen, the gilded splendour of the 'gingerbread work' of all classes of warship was typical of the extravagance of the age, and a reminder to the world of the glory of the King.

DUTCH HERO

Michiel Adriaanszoon de Ruyter (1607-1676) was the greatest Dutch naval hero of the 17th century. He was a veteran of campaigns against Spain, France and Sweden and led three wars against England. His most famous exploit was the daring raid on Chatham, England's principal naval base, in 1667. On this occasion his men captured or burnt 16 ships and they took the pride of England's fleet, the *Royal Charles* back to Holland. De Ruyter was mortally wounded nine years later, fighting the French off Sicily.

The Great Age of Sail

The long series of wars from the 1750s up to 1815 created many great naval heroes. In parallel with Britain's expanding trading economy, the British navy gradually emerged as the dominant power among sea-faring nations, winning her country the position it was to enjoy during the 19th century as 'ruler of the waves'. But this success story was not all smooth sailing. American privateers ravaged British trade in the War of Independence, and though America's new navy had few ships, these won several single ship actions in the War of 1812.

BOARDERS AWAY!

In close action, boarding parties were often used. With two ships locked together, a strong force of marines would charge onto the enemy's upper deck. A well-disciplined attack could force a surrender in just minutes; the enemy crew were trapped below deck, while control was seized above. Nelson first found fame when he used this tactic to capture two major Spanish warships in ten minutes.

BELLONA, A CLASSIC 74-GUN SHIP

This model shows some features of a late 18th-century ship-of-the-line. Officers' quarters were in the stern; in battle the furniture was cleared and the cabins dismantled, leaving the decks free to work the broadside guns. With its windows and decorative carving, the stern was the most vulnerable part of the ship, with few strong timbers to resist an enemy's fire.

The copper cladding on this ship below the waterline was a secret weapon. Copper armoured ships against destructive wood-boring molluscs and algae. Weeds on the hulls of timber ships would grow so long they would create 'drag' and slow down the vessel; copperclad ships remained as fast and streamlined as when they left the dockyard.

'HOT PRESS'

The strict discipline, low pay and long service made going to sea very unpopular. Needing manpower, navies resorted to impressment; the much-feared Press Gangs could forcibly enlist anyone with seafaring experience.

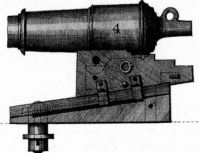

'DEATH OF NELSON'

In an age of great naval heroes - Anson, St Vincent, Suffren, John Paul Jones and many others - Horatio Nelson was the greatest and is still the most popular. This ornament is just one example of the hundreds of souvenirs made to mark his victories - and his death at Trafalgar on 21 October 1805. On the anniversary of the battle, the British Navy still toasts 'The Immortal Memory of Nelson'.

Nelson

THE LINE OF BATTLE

In the 18th and early 19th centuries, decades of war at sea and constant blockade of enemy ports made the British, in particular, hardened seamen and shiphandlers. A battle line of warships in perfect formation was a thrilling and formidable sight.

THE SMASHING CARRONADE

Introduced in the 1780s, this lightweight gun fired a heavy ball and needed only three or four crew, compared up to fifteen required to operate a 'long' gun. But this gun was only accurate at short range ship armed only with carronades had to run the gauntlet of long range gunfire to close to point blank range. But once at close quarters the heavier carronade ball, and high rate of fire, packed a brutal punch. The effect was so devastating that the gun was nicknamed 'the Smasher'.

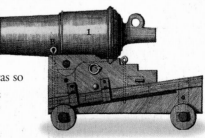

Full Steam Ahead

The navies of the world were slow to adopt steam power for their warships, preferring to wait for the new technology to prove itself. Merchant shipowners, however, were quick to exploit steam, and its independence from wind and tide. The United States was first to build a steam warship, a twin-hulled floating battery for defending New York harbour. Designed by Robert Fulton, the *Demologus* or *Fulton's No. 1* was completed in 1815. The British navy began to test steam-paddle warships in the 1830s. But by the 1840s the screw propeller had thoroughly proved itself in a series of tests. The most famous demonstration was made by the screw sloop *Rattler,* when she towed the otherwise identical paddle vessel *Alecto* backwards at 2.7 knots, as both ships steamed full ahead. The arrival of screw propulsion meant that the full potential of steam power could now be put to use, and the first iron-hulled warships were soon in service. Naval warfare was being swept up in the changes brought about by the Industrial Revolution.

BOMBARDMENT

Despite their side paddle-wheels being prone to damage by enemy fire, small steam ships were occasionally used to tow larger sail-powered warships in battle. At the bombardment of Sebastopol during the Crimean War (1854-1856), steam frigates were lashed alongside the battleships, to help manoeuvre the big sailing ships.

HMS *RHADAMANTHUS*

This model shows clearly why paddle wheels were not suitable for warships. Aside from the risk of being disabled by enemy fire, the wheels reduced the space available for mounting broadside cannons. The screw propeller had neither of these disadvantages.

THE *DIANA*

The first steamship to be used in action, and the first to fire rockets in battle, was the East India Company's steamer *Diana*, during British operations against Burmese pirates in 1824. Originally intended just for towing sailing ships, the British Navy fitted her with Congreve rocket tubes. This small ship can claim to be the distant ancestor of today's guided missile cruisers.

RIG OF THE DAY

Uniform clothing for seamen was first issued by the British Navy in the 1850s, over a century after the introduction of officers' uniform in 1748. Seamen traditionally wore loose-fitting trousers, baggy jumpers and short jackets, with a characteristic straw hat and blue collar. The new regulations merely made this style official, as this group at the double wheel of a battleship shows.

THE SCREW

The screw propeller would not be used for the whole sea voyage. When the wind was favourable ships saved coal by going under sail. The idle propeller had to be moved, to stop it causing drag and delaying the ship. This model was made to demonstrate how the screw could be raised out of the water, into a well in the hull.

A HIDDEN THREAT

Moored mines guarding the approaches to harbours were first used during the Crimean War, which also saw fighting in the Baltic, the White Sea and the Pacific, as well as the Black Sea. The new Russian 'infernal machines' – or 'torpedoes', as they were called – would cause some damage to any ships that triggered one, but the gunpower charge was too small to be really dangerous.

SCREW LINE-OF-BATTLE SHIP

Outwardly little different to a purely sailing warship, this cutaway diagram shows the internal layout of a large steam warship.

THE LIFTING SCREW

When changing over from steam power to sails, the order '*Down funnel, up screw!*' would be given. It took the whole crew to hoist the heavy bronze propeller.

BULKY BOILERS

Much of the hold had to be given up to boilers, engines and coal, leaving little storage space for provisions.

CLASH OF IRON

The first battle between ironclads ended in stalemate. The fight took place between the Confederate *Virginia* and the Union's *Monitor* in March 1862 during the American Civil War. The *Virginia*, previously the USS *Merrimack*, was a steam frigate converted to an ironclad; *Monitor*, with her revolutionary revolving gun turret, was built to the design of the inventor John Ericsson. Neither ship was entirely seaworthy or effective.

BREECH LOADER

An American naval gun at the Battle of Santiago 1898. Progress in the use of metals and in engineering made breech-loading rifled guns like this the winners in the gun versus armour race. Improved propellant charges, shell design and recoil systems gave the new lighter guns greater accuracy at longer ranges and a higher rate of fire. Nevertheless, navies were slow to adapt to the new technology.

DEVASTATING PIONEER

A step toward the true battleship, the *Devastation* of 1872 was the first truly seagoing warship with no masts or sails, relying on steam power alone. Her iron hull was armoured and she carried her 12-inch muzzle loading guns in centreline turrets, not on the broadside.

FRENCH STYLE

French warship design followed its own path during the last quarter of the 19th century. The barbette ship *Le Furieux* shows the typical 'tumblehome', or inward sloping, of her heavily-armoured sides.

GATLING GUN

In the 1880s, the hand-cranked gatling gun was adopted by several navies and fitted in large warships as a defence against torpedo boat attack: it was also used by naval shore parties in campaigns on land. A century later, close-in weapon systems featuring multi-barrelled automatic guns are again being fitted in warships to defend against the modern equivalent of the torpedo boat, the sea-skimming missile.

Ironclad Ships

The Battle of Sinope in 1853, in which a Russian squadron utterly destroyed a Turkish fleet of wooden ships with explosive shellfire, was the single event that convinced the world's navies that iron should be the ship-building material of the future. The lesson was reinforced by the damage shells inflicted on French and British ships in shore bombardments during the Crimean War. The French Navy was first to launch an ironclad frigate, the *Gloire*, in 1859. Her structure was traditional oak, but her sides were armoured with 5-inch iron plates. The design revolution was completed a year later, by the British HMS *Warrior*. Built entirely of iron and armoured over a teak backing, she and her sister HMS *Black Prince* outclassed any other ship afloat. With improvements in gun-making techniques and the increasingly powerful performance of steam engines, the naval arms race was on! Naval tactics were updated to take these new technologies into account. Britain maintained the largest navy – outnumbering the combined forces of her two biggest rivals.

JOURNEY'S END

During the Russo-Japanese War (1904-1905), a Russian fleet made a seven-month voyage from the Baltic to Japan. They should have stayed at home! Admiral Togo's skillful fleet overwhelmed them and the war ended in Japanese victory.

ADMIRAL TOGO

Following the opening of Japan to the West in the 1860s, Heihachiro Togo (1847-1934) received his early naval training in Britain. He became commander-in-chief of the Japanese Grand Fleet in 1904. In his flagship *Mikasa* (left), he led his fleet to crushing victories over the Russians at Round Island and Tsu Shima, establishing Japan as a modern naval power.

Early Submarines

Inventors and scientists of early generations were faced with an enormous challenge trying to unlock and conquer the secrets of the oceans. As they put the first tentative toe into the water, they had little understanding of the element and its physical properties - how it changes with depth; how it varies in density between fresh and salt water; and the treacherous sub-surface currents. Through a variety of dangerous experiments, they slowly but surely pushed back the frontiers of knowledge. Counteracting the craft's buoyancy and getting it beneath the surface; keeping water out; refreshing the air to avoid suffocating the crew; propelling it underwater - these were all practical problems that had to be overcome with only the most basic materials of wood and leather available to work with. Nevertheless they persevered, and by the eighteenth century goatskin had given way to metal hoops for strength, and the oar had been replaced by the crankshaft and the propeller for propulsion. The submarine design that we know was beginning to take shape.

THE FIRST OCEAN VOYAGE

Simon Lake's *Argonaut* (USA) can claim to have been the first submarine ever to make an ocean voyage, when in 1898 it travelled under its own power through November storms from Norfolk, Virginia, to New York - a remarkable feat. From it Lake developed a military version, *Protector*, several of which were sold to Russia in 1906.

THE TURTLE ATTACKS

The first submarine attack in naval history took place in New York harbour, in 1776, during the American War of Independence. The *Turtle*, designed by David Bushnell, came remarkably close to sinking its target. It carried a detachable mine which was intended to be drilled into the wooden bottom of the British target ship, HMS *Eagle*. Because of an impenetrable metal plate on the underside of the ship, the mission was not a success.

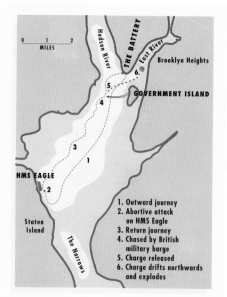

0   1   2
MILES

THE BATTERY
Hudson River
East River
Brooklyn Heights
GOVERNMENT ISLAND
HMS EAGLE
Staten Island
The Narrows

1. Outward journey
2. Abortive attack on HMS Eagle
3. Return journey
4. Chased by British military barge
5. Charge released
6. Charge drifts northwards and explodes

NINE BRAVE MEN

The first submarine to sink another warship was the CSS *Hunley* when in 1864, during the American Civil War, she successfully attacked the USS *Housatonic*. Eight men and the captain were cramped into a tiny space, turning a long crankshaft. They paid a heavy price for their efforts.

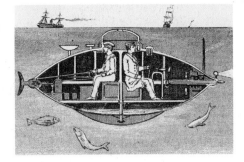

THE LITTLE *GOUBET*

This tiny submarine was the first to be powered by electricity. The basic concept was that it could be carried by a battleship and set down within its range of target. Although beset by problems, it had sufficient merit to be bought by Brazil for £10,000.

THE *HUNLEY'S* TORPEDO

The torpedo was a large mine on a harpoon spar that had to be rammed against the target's wooden side. The explosion should have occurred once the submarine had backed away, but unfortunately it went off too early. The *Hunley* was swamped by the blast and she sank with all her crew.

GARRETT'S *RESURGAM*

Until 1879 every submarine that put to sea was propelled by man's muscle power in some form or other, then an English clergyman, Reverend William Garrett, introduced a steam engine into his vessel, *Resurgam*. The world's first mechanical submarine was born and gone were the days of oars and paddles! Garrett's dream was to surround the British Isles with dozens of his submarines as protection against any potential aggressor. Although his design was not accepted by the British Admiralty, it did catch the eye of a number of other navies. Garrett teamed up with a Swedish businessman, Thorsten Nordenfelt, and together they built a number of steam driven submarines for Germany, Greece and Turkey. These vessels were not successful however and, like many great inventors, Garrett was to die penniless. He did find brief fame in the Near East, and he is shown opposite in the uniform of a Turkish Navy Commander!

SUBMARINES IN ANCIENT TIMES

Medieval manuscripts tell of Alexander the Great being lowered in a glass barrel where he remained on the bottom of the sea for some time, and on surfacing described the wonderful things he had seen. He is reputed to have used manned submersibles in Tyre harbour in 332 BC in order to defend his ships from divers who were attempting to cut their anchor ropes. But it was to be another eighteen centuries before the idea of submersible ships was discussed again.

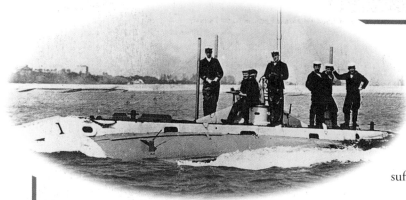

HOLLAND 1

In 1901 the British Navy adopted the design of the *Holland Class* for its first experimental submarines. *Holland 1* is pictured here at sea with seven of the eight crew on the casing (upper deck). Note the lack of a conning tower - it is easy to see why these little submarines suffered flooding during a storm!

A STEEL FISH

In 1898 a report in the New York Journal, read *'STEEL FISH WITH REVOLVING TAIL WILL PROTECT OUR HARBOUR - The Holland Submarine Terror, the Newest Wonder of Naval Science, Which Lives and Swims Under Water and Noiselessly and Unseen Creeps Up Under an Enemy's Side, Hurling Into It Thunderbolts of Dynamite from its Torpedo Guns'.*

CONTROL CENTRE

This cutaway of *Holland 1* shows that a great deal of technical progress was made in only three years from *Holland's* first design. The Control Room was from where the submarine was steered when submerged.

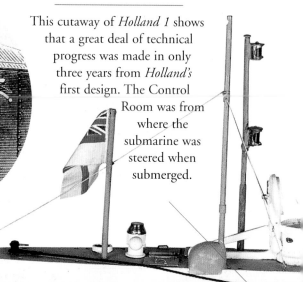

THE PROPULSION TRAIN

The gasoline (petrol) engine could only power the submarine on the surface. It was connected to the motor, shaft and propeller to drive the submarine along at about 10 knots. The engine also charged the battery which provided the energy to turn the motor when the submarine was submerged. A speed of 7 knots could be reached and maintained for about five hours before the battery was exhausted.

INSIDE THE FISH

The reporter from the New York Journal drew a number of images of the craft, which clearly show that the earliest form of navigation was the Captain looking out of a porthole, standing on a soapbox, with a member of the crew having to lie down to get past him.

The *Holland*

The first wholly successful submarine in history was the *Holland* or as it was known in the United States Navy in 1900, the *Adder*. Because it was powered by one of the recently invented internal combustion engines burning gasoline (petrol), the submarine's inventor, John Philip Holland, was able to make his design smaller and much more habitable than a steam driven equivalent. This engine was coupled to an electric generator to recharge the batteries that in turn supplied the electric motor that propelled the submarine when it was submerged. In the bow was a launch tube for one of the new Whitehead torpedoes. Most important of all, Holland knew how to make a submarine behave properly, with the capability of submerging or surfacing rapidly on command, and of remaining level when running at depth under water.

THE FIRST DESIGNS

John Philip Holland, the inventor of the modern submarine, was an American of Irish birth. He was a brilliant designer and spent many of his early years building submarines that were intended to attack ships in New York Harbour! In 1898 he created the blueprint for the mother of all submarines afloat today. The efficient use of the internal combustion engine and electric motor to power the craft produced the first successful long distance submarine.

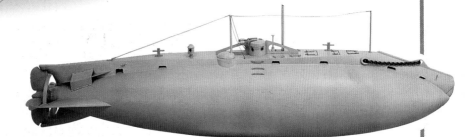

THE TORPEDO TUBE

The great advance in torpedo technology occurred in 1868 when the British engineer, Sir Robert Whitehead, flew the world's first locomotive torpedo. He was also the grandfather of the Von Trapp Singers *(The Sound of Music)*! The torpedo was expelled from the tube by high pressure air. It only had a range of about 300 metres, so the submarine had to get close to its target to be successful.

THE MOTHER SHIP

This model of *Holland 1* shows a remarkable resemblance to a whale, and explains why the design was so successful. Although submarines have become bigger and more powerful, the basic principles have always remained the same.

Submarines: Up to 1913

Submarining in Edwardian times was a rough, ready, rude and ruthless way of life, whose impact on the social structure of the British Navy was revolutionary. Never before had officers and men served and lived so closely together, sharing the inherent dangers and also the crudest sanitary arrangements (buckets!). Of dangers there were many - exploding petrol engines; collision; flooding; - and submariners in many navies lost their lives in accidents. However technology and safety (but not comfort) slowly improved. Petrol engines gave way to diesel (a safer fuel); internal bulkheads were introduced to limit flooding; higher conning towers provided protection against rough seas; size and strength of hulls increased; periscopes, and thus the safety lookout, were vastly improved. By the out-break of the Great War, the submarine, though viewed as a defensive weapon, was established in every major fleet world-wide.

FRENCH PIONEERS

The French were great submarine pioneers but, because they began their design programme many years before JP Holland in the USA, they were unable to adapt quickly to new technology.
In 1901 they introduced twenty small submarines including *Dorade*, as defence mobiles' for a number of ports. Their petrol driven engines soon proved hazardous, so the submarines had to re-charge their batteries when alongside, greatly limiting their range. They carried their two torpedoes on the outside, unlike other submarines which carried theirs internally.

THREE WHITE MICE

One of the most dangerous exhaust products of a petrol engine is the gas carbon monoxide, which has no smell. Exhaust from the engine was designed to be expelled through a mast, but it would often creep into the boat threatening to asphyxiate the crew. A mouse, which has only a small body weight would quickly react to a leak by becoming unconscious. If one collapsed, the submarine quickly surfaced for fresh air.

JAPANESE OFFICER'S CEREMONIAL SWORD

Despite the crude conditions onboard submarines, all the crew would have a full uniform to wear when ashore or on ceremonial occasions.
The Imperial Japanese Navy, which introduced *Holland Class* submarines in 1904, was no exception. The rise of the Japanese Navy was remarkable, reaching in decades a level of skill which had taken many other nations centuries to achieve. Always at the forefront of technology Japan, during the Russo-Japanese war, was the first nation in history to use successfully the torpedo in anger.

YES TO SUBMARINES

When the submarine was first introduced into the United States there was a lot of general unease about its presence. Lieutenant Larry H Caldwell (seen here with his crew on board the first American submarine in June 1901) was a respected Officer who could foresee the future strengths of the submarine. He became a pioneer for the acceptance of such a fighting force into the Navy despite opposition.

FAST AND DANGEROUS

In 1916, the Royal Navy introduced a steam submarine capable of providing support to surface warships. Known as the 'fleet escort' submarine, it was eventually designated the K-class and 18 were built. In order to be effective, the submarine had to be able to travel at 24 knots when surfaced. This could not be achieved by diesel engines, so steam was used to power the engines making them the fastest submarines around (until nuclear powered submarines were invented). The K's were the most hazardous submarines ever introduced and eight suffered accidents, killing a large number of their crews.

HOME COMFORTS

Of all men-of-war the submarine is the least self-supporting when not actively employed at sea. Every aspect of life on board points to the necessity for a base for both the boat and the crew when they are in harbour. Shore Bases and Depot Ships serve this purpose. *Acheron,* a German ship, was a typical example of an early Depot Ship, that could provide the basic amenities of a bed and a bath. Later Depot Ships could also go to sea and provide mobile dockyard support.

INSIDE A SUBMARINE

This shows the need for comfort when not at sea! Several men would call this cramped space home, and cheek by jowl with the torpedoes they would eat, sleep, write their letters home and generally conduct their lives. Privacy was non existent, and the need to get on well together was of paramount importance. The torpedo tubes in the background were an ever present statement of the job they were expected to do, and reminded them constantly of the danger they faced together. At 'Action Stations' the table and seat lockers would be folded away.

World War I (1914~18)

The underlying causes of the First World War were complex and, even now, are not entirely understood. At that time most of the major European countries were busy acquiring colonies around the world. The leaders of each country mistrusted the others and so a series of alliances were drawn up to achieve an even balance of power and prevent any one country from becoming too powerful. The spark that began the conflict occurred in 1914 when the heir to the Austrian throne, Archduke Franz Ferdinand, was assassinated. The Austrians blamed the Serbians and declared war on them. Russia went to Serbia's aid and Germany to Austria's. Germany had already been undergoing an armament programme and began to flex its muscles, initially to establish itself as the dominant power in Europe with little thought of an ongoing international conflict. However, when Germany invaded Belgium, which had been neutral until then, a threat was posed to Britain's maritime security and so Britain entered the war. Soon after, the conflict escalated into a world-wide conflict.

AMERICA ENTERS THE WAR

In the early stages of the war, German U-boats observed the international code of not sinking ships on sight, without warning. In February 1917 they ceased to do so, which threatened American shipping in the Atlantic. America had been supplying the allies and was forced to enter the conflict. Germany had hoped to defeat Britain before the U.S. could mobilise its strength, but seriously miscalculated events. Germany formally surrendered on 11 November 1918 and signed armistice agreements dictated by the allies.

GAS ATTACKS

When the war reached a stalemate position in the trenches, desperate measures were introduced to win the upper hand, including showering the enemy with poisonous gas canisters, such as mustard gas, which was a powerful irritant and caused severe burning. Soldiers had to wear cumbersome respirator masks as protection. Many died or suffered life-long respiratory problems as a result of even brief exposure to such gases.

CIVILIAN ARMY

The allied army consisted largely of untrained civilians and was initially no match for the German army. Britain, like other countries in Europe, had become complacent, and was unprepared when war was declared. Rising unemployment throughout Europe, however, meant that there was no shortage of volunteers, but there were serious shortages of materials, especially munitions. Women were forced to work in factories, shipyards and even the armed services to help with the war effort, in all the allied countries.

Lettre d'un "Poilu"

Sans cesse, ton papa, ma fille bien-aimée,
Baise ta chère image, en mon âme enfermée.

AERIAL WARFARE

World War I saw the first successful use of prolonged aerial attack in an armed conflict. Machine guns were mounted above the cockpits and bombs were dropped over the side, taking the fight beyond the range of land-based or ship-based guns. Aeroplanes were also used to spy on enemy positions.

DEATH IN THE TRENCHES

Following the military deadlock after the Battle of the Somme, both sides dug themselves into trenches. Life in the trenches was inhospitable, wet and cold, and caused the war to drag on far longer than the six weeks most had expected the conflict to last. Complicated tunnels and dugouts were constructed with each side periodically going 'over the top' to attack the enemy lines under constant fire. Loss of life was horrendously high for very little strategic gain and many of those who survived suffered ill-health for the remainder of their lives.

MASS DESTRUCTION

For the first time in history, during World War I, the mass destruction of entire communities became possible, largely as a result of the massive new guns then being manufactured. Heavy guns, with a range of up to 60 miles, could bombard towns from a safe distance. Despite this, the basic tactics of the generals in World War I were the same as they had always been, in ranging armies in front of each other. The power of the weapons used, however, resulted in much higher casualty figures. Over 10 million people lost their lives in the conflict.

TANK WARFARE

Armoured cars had been used since at least 1904. But, the idea of completely encasing guns in heavily-armoured vehicles driven on caterpillar treads and able to traverse any terrain, was developed by a British Royal Engineer, Lt. Colonel Ernest Swinton. They were first used on the Somme in 1916 and then at the Battle of Cambrai the following year.

Submarines in WWI

It was during WWI amid great controversy that the submarine came of age as a weapon system. Britain has always relied on the sea lanes for vital supplies, so the Germans used their U-boats against her merchant shipping to starve the country into submission. This proved that the submarine could be used as an effective weapon. Between 1914-1918, the most successful German U-boat, U-35, managed to sink 324 merchant ships. Then in 1917 the Allies started to sail their merchant ships in convoys protected by a warship escort. This greatly reduced their number of ships lost through submarine attack. The convoy system and the entry of the United States into the war kept the essential lifeline across the Atlantic open.

At this time, there was no means available to detect a submarine other than from visual look-out, since ASDIC (sound detection) was invented after the war.

A DANGEROUS LIFE

The mine was possibly the greatest hazard faced by a submarine crew. Unseen, undetectable, and unpredictable, this devastating weapon accounted for hundreds of submariners' lives during both World Wars. The young men here from HMS *E34* not only suffered extreme discomfort at sea, but their lives were snuffed out in an instant when they touched the horn of an enemy mine in the Heligoland Bight in 1918.

SENDING MESSAGES

Until the introduction of wireless telegraphy into submarines in 1916, the signalman had to rely on Semaphore flags, pigeon post and the Aldis Lamp as methods of exchanging messages. Wireless telegraphy, with an eventual radius of 100 miles, provided up-to-date information from ashore.

TURKISH BLUNDER-BUSS

British submarines operated extensively during the Dardanelles campaign against the Turks, who were German allies. One misty morning a lone Turkish fisherman came across HMS *E12* charging her batteries on the surface. In sheer fright he let loose his blunderbuss at the grey monster. His punishment was the loss of his gun - but he was given a brandy in compensation and set free.

THE LOOKOUT

When travelling on the surface, it was essential for a submarine to maintain a vigilant look-out in order to find its target and avoid being surprised. In rough weather this was a cold and wet duty. These lookouts on the bridge of a U-boat, dressed in oilskins, are well protected from the elements in order to conduct their search of the horizon. One of their shipmates has just finished his period of watch and is escaping to relative comfort below. In the cat and mouse game of submarining, it was kill or be killed - with no room for error.

THE *LUSITANIA*

The event that brought home the appalling consequences of submarine warfare was the unlawful sinking of the Cunard Liner, *Lusitania*, by the German submarine *U-20* in May 1915. Nearly 1200 lives were lost including many women and children. This grave error of judgement weakened United States resolve to remain neutral in the war, since a number of the *Lusitania's* passengers were American. A propaganda medal was struck in Germany to celebrate the 'success'.

THE FACE OF A SHARK

Submarines had to enter dry-dock occasionally to have their underwater fittings overhauled. The two port torpedo tubes of this German *U-162* can be seen with the bow caps open, and behind them are the bow shutters that completed the streamlining of the hull when they were shut. The serrated device on the bow was designed to cut mooring wires of any mines encountered. From this angle the submarine more resembles a shark than a whale.

NAVIGATION

The sextant was a device used in astro (heavenly)-navigation, the basic principle of which was to measure angles of the sun, stars and planets, which when converted into bearing lines, provided a position on the earth's surface. Often it was the only means of navigating, but if there was constant cloud cover a submarine could go for days without being able to 'fix' its position. This could, and occasionally did, have disastrous consequences particularly with respect to avoiding known minefields, or straying out of its defined patrol area where it was safe from friendly fire.

The First Fighters

In 1903 the Wright Brothers made the first successful aeroplane flights in the USA. Seven years later, the British Secretary of State for War said, *'We do not consider that aeroplanes will be of any possible use for war purposes.'* This view was held by officials around the world, including in France which rapidly became the centre of aviation pioneering. However, in 1912 the British military formed the Royal Flying Corps (RFC), to fly reconnaissance missions to see what enemy troops were doing. Just for fun, the pilots began firing at kites with rifles and revolvers. By 1913 one of the first military aircraft was put on display by the giant Vickers company. Called the 'Experimental Fighting Biplane', it was specially designed so that a machine gun could be mounted in the nose. When war broke out in Europe in August 1914, Vickers were contracted to produce 50 of their FB.5s and by 1915 over 100 had been sent to France with the RFC squadrons, primarily instructed to ram any Zeppelins encountered on their way. Without parachutes, this was not an exciting prospect for the untrained pilots, who resourcefully wore car tyres in case they came down in the English Channel. Before long two-seater planes were carrying observers with rifles and revolvers trained on the enemy, and combat aircraft became a reality. All this must have been a great shock to the Generals and politicians who had written off aeroplanes as useless in wartime.

ZEPPELIN AIRSHIPS

Before the First World War began in 1914 the idea of aeroplanes in war was remote, but the use of airships was a possibility. Both the German Army and Navy used airships, and from 1915 they used them to drop bombs on Britain. It took aeroplanes to shoot them down.

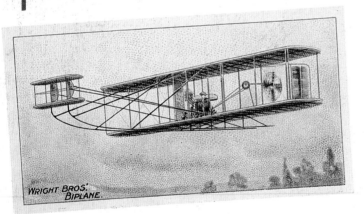

WRIGHT BROS. BIPLANE.

WRIGHT BIPLANE

In August 1910 Lt Jake Fickel, of the US Army, flew as passenger in a Wright biplane and fired four shots from a Springfield rifle at a target almost one metre (3 feet) square on the ground. He scored two hits. He was the first man ever to fire a gun from an aeroplane.

EXPÉRIENCES DE LANCEMENT DE BOMBES EN AÉROPLANE

THE FRENCH AIR CORPS

This illustration depicts early manoeuvres by the French Air Corps in 1913, showing them dropping bombs from aeroplanes.

VICKERS GUNBUS

In February 1913 what could be called the first British military aircraft was put on display by Vickers at an Aero Show in London. This 'Experimental Fighting Biplane' (EFB) had quite a short central body (a 'nacelle') with the engine at the back driving a pusher propeller. This meant that the tail had to be attached by four thin rods (called booms), which were far enough apart to leave room for the propeller. This rather strange arrangement was adopted so that the company's own Vickers-Maxim machine gun could be mounted in the nose, fed by a long belt of ammunition. It was aimed by a gunner in the front cockpit. Just behind him was the pilot. This 'pusher' arrangement was later used by many types of aircraft, including the FB.5 (Fighting Biplane, type 5), popularly called the Gunbus, which was active in the First World War.

THE PILOT'S SIDEARM

After the War began most reconnaissance pilots carried a personal 'sidearm', for possible use to avoid capture after being shot down. This Webley pistol was a favourite for British pilots.

GUNBUS COCKPIT

Pilots soon discovered that they needed instruments to help them fly. The first were a tachometer (showing how fast the engine was turning), an altimeter (showing how high the aeroplane was flying), and an airspeed indicator (showing speed through the air).

Dawn of Air Warfare

DROPPING BOMBS

The first bombers were often ordinary aircraft fitted with a bomb-dropping mechanism invented and fitted on the spot. An even simpler answer was for the crew to hang the bombs beside the cockpits and drop them by hand.

In 1912 the British Government decided that perhaps aeroplanes might have some military use. They organized a competition, entered by Geoffrey de Havilland with his B.E.1. Although he did not win, he continued to improve his neat biplane which became the Royal Flying Corps' most numerous type in the First World War. It was a B.E. that was to claim the first air combat victory on 25 August 1914, only three weeks after the start of the War. Three B.E.2s chased a German aircraft for miles before the German pilot, realizing he could not get away, landed in a field. Both occupants escaped to a nearby wood. The British pilots ran after them, brandishing pistols, but returned to set fire to the enemy aircraft and then took off again. A month later, Frenchman Sergeant Joseph Frantz suddenly came up behind a German Aviatik. His Voisin plane was armed with a Hotchkiss machine gun. Quickly his observer, Corporal Louis Quénault, aimed at the enemy aircraft and shot it down. This was the first aircraft actually shot down in air warfare, and the dawn of the aeroplane as a weapon of war.

MACHINE GUN

It was the machine gun that transformed aeroplanes into fighters. In the First World War almost all the machine guns fitted to aircraft were originally designed for use by soldiers on the ground. Many French aircraft used this type of Hotchkiss machine gun, mounted on pivots and aimed by the observer. He was usually in a cockpit behind the pilot, but in the Voisin he was in front.

THE 'BLERIOT EXPERIMENTAL' OR B.E.2

Louis Blériot was a Frenchman who made monoplanes, but his name became synonymous with the RFC for aeroplanes with a propeller on the nose. De Havilland's B.E.2 was popular with the RFC. It was very stable in flight, which meant it could fly without the pilot touching the controls. Therefore both pilot and observer could watch the battlefield below and write down anything of interest.

This stability made the aircraft difficult to manoeuvre, which was disastrous against the new German planes in the First World War.

NATIONAL MARKINGS c.1915

Once the War began it was soon realized that aircraft had to be painted with a clear indication of their nationality, so ground soldiers did not shoot at their own aircraft. Soon simple national markings were devised.

Great Britain   *Russia*   *Belgium*   *Italy*   *Germany*

MONOPLANE FIGHTERS

The British thought monoplanes unsafe, but the French Morane-Saulnier firm made them in large numbers. This Type L monoplane had the wing passing through the fuselage (body), while other Moranes had it fixed above the fuselage on struts.

The Fokker Scourge

FOKKER EINDECKER

In 1915-16 these highly manoeuvrable little monoplanes struck fear into the hearts of Allied aviators. They so dominated the skies over the Western Front that the British aircraft, such as the B.E.2s, were called 'Fokker fodder'. Later in 1916 they faded from the scene, because aircraft were becoming stronger and more powerful.

Even before the start of the First World War several far-sighted people had come to the conclusion that the best way for an aeroplane to shoot down an enemy would be for it to have a machine gun fixed to fire straight ahead. It would be aimed by manoeuvring the whole aircraft. Thus, the pilot need be the only person on board, and the aircraft could be smaller and more agile than a two-seater. Of course, with the propeller at the front there was a problem. The French pilot, Roland Garros, just fixed strong steel deflectors to the propeller of his Morane L monoplane at the beginning of the War and quickly destroyed four German aircraft. When Garros was himself shot down, the Germans discovered his idea, and asked Anthony Fokker to copy it. Fokker came up with something better – he invented a way to synchronize the gun to the speed of the propeller, so it only fired when there was no propeller blade in front. The result was the Fokker Eindecker. Though it was a low-powered little aircraft, its combination of adequate speed, excellent manoeuvrability and a forward-firing machine gun made it deadly.

GERMANY'S TOP ACES

Here Baron von Richthofen, Germany's top ace, is surrounded by four of his pilots. When flying, they often left their caps behind but kept on their cavalry boots and heavy leather greatcoats in order to try to keep warm. Their counterparts in the RFC wore a strange double-breasted tunic (popularly called a 'maternity jacket'), and increasingly wore specially designed calf-length soft boots lined with thick fur.

FOKKER TRIPLANE

Officially called the Dr.I, the brightly painted triplanes were as feared as the Eindecker had been previously. Allied planes were usually camouflaged, or just painted a dull olive-brown, but the best German fighters were organized into large groups called circuses, in which each pilot could choose to paint his aircraft in an individual scheme of vivid colours to frighten the enemy. This scarlet one is a replica of that used by the greatest of them all, Baron Manfred von Richthofen (the Red Baron). He held Germany's top-score of 80 victories when he was shot down and killed in April 1918.

ANTHONY FOKKER

Anthony Fokker was a Dutchman, but before the First World War he set up his aircraft factory near Berlin. By the end of the War he was famous (British people would say infamous), and he had no difficulty in moving his factory to his native Amsterdam, where he made everything from fighters to airliners.

D.H.2

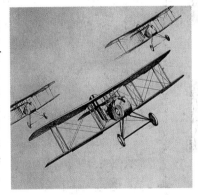

Captain Geoffrey de Havilland was one of the most famous British aircraft designers. In 1915 he designed the D.H.2, with a single cockpit in the nose fitted with a machine gun. The D.H.2 was a useful single-seater, but it was the later D.H.4, with its 375-horsepower engine, that became the Allies' most important anti-Zeppelin aircraft.

NIEUPORT XI

The French Nieuport company made some of the best single-seat fighters of their day. The Nie. XI was called *Le Bébé* because it was so small. It had only an 80-horsepower engine and weighed little more than 454 kg (1,000 lb). They were outstandingly agile biplanes that could easily catch the Fokkers and beat them in close combat.

Killing Machines

By 1916 air warfare was an accomplished fact. As well as the task of reconnaissance, aircraft had been developed to drop bombs, aim torpedoes at ships and, not least, shoot down other aircraft. Combat aircraft were at first called 'fighting scouts', but they gradually became known as 'fighters' (except in the USA where until the Second World War they were called 'pursuits'). The key to success in air combat was higher flight performance: faster speed, more rapid climb to greater altitudes, and ever-better ability to manoeuvre. These demands could only be met by fitting more powerful engines. Armaments were also important and many were developed during the First World War. Dozens of different small bombs were tried, and showers of darts. A few pilots even tried to snare enemy aircraft with grappling hooks at the end of a long cable! Night fighters also made their first appearance because of a need to find some aerial defence against German Zeppelin airships.

Armed with a crew, machine guns, an electric generator and a searchlight, they were too slow to be effective. Ordinary fighters were better, and in 1919 the best was the Fokker D.VII. Not particularly special, but extraordinarily effective, the Allies demanded the hand-over of every D.VII after the War.

TAKING AIM

On this British fighter, the S.E.5a (S.E. meant 'scout experimental'), there are two types of gunsight – a ring-and-bead sight on the left used for close range, and an Aldis sight on the right, which contained lenses to see longer distances. There was a Vickers machine gun installed inside the nose, and on a special mounting above the upper wing was a drum-fed Lewis machine gun (above).

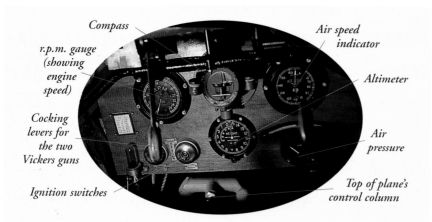

Compass

r.p.m. gauge (showing engine speed)

Cocking levers for the two Vickers guns

Ignition switches

Air speed indicator

Altimeter

Air pressure

Top of plane's control column

CAMEL COCKPIT

Most successful of all British fighters was the Sopwith Camel. It was said that looking ahead from a Camel cockpit was the most exciting view in the world, partly because the pilot looked over his two Vickers machine guns. By this time fighter cockpits had more instruments. The ignition switches were clumsy circular units with brass covers exactly like light switches in 1916 houses.

DOGFIGHT

By 1917 it was common for dozens of aircraft to engage in what became called 'a dogfight'. Each pilot tried to get on the tail of an enemy in order to shoot him down, whilst at the same time preventing any other enemy from getting on his own tail. Thus, he needed eyes in the back of his head. Here a Spad of RFC No. 23 Squadron tries to get on the tail of a Fokker D.VII marked with the simpler black cross which Germany introduced in 1918.

SPAD XIII

In 1915 French aircraft designer Louis Bechereau decided to use a completely new engine made by the Hispano-Suiza company (the name means 'Spanish-Swiss' and is better known as a car manufacturer). It had eight water-cooled cylinders in two rows and gave 150 horsepower. The result was an excellent fighter called Spad VII, and 5,600 were made. Next came the Spad XIII, with the engine uprated to 220 horsepower, armed with two Vickers guns. No fewer than 8,472 were made by 1918.

BRISTOL FIGHTER

Officially called the Bristol F.2B, this was unusual in that it was a successful fighter with a crew of two. In both World Wars, the way to shoot down an enemy was to get 'on his tail' and get the hostile aircraft in one's gunsight. While the Bristol pilot did this, the observer in the rear cockpit had either one or two Lewis machine guns which he could aim anywhere to the rear.

LEWIS MACHINE GUN

This gun was ideal for use by observers (backseaters), because it worked well even on its side or upside down, and was fed by a drum on top (holding either 47 or 97 rounds). Drums could be changed in seconds, the empty drum often being thrown overboard. The barrel was inside a fat casing containing cooling fins.

BRITISH BULLDOG

HMS *Warspite* was launched in 1913 and served in both World Wars. She earned battle honours in no fewer than 14 major actions including the Battle of Jutland (1916) and the D-Day landings (1944). Her bulldog mascot matches her fighting style – she never gave up.

SMS *HELGOLAND*

The *Helgoland* (right) was typical of German battleships built just before World War I. Like the *Dreadnought* she was an 'all-big-gun' ship, mounting twelve 12-inch guns in six twin turrets, and was clothed in up to 12 inches of steel armour plate.

The Age of the Battleship

RECORD-BREAKERS

The Japanese battleships *Musashi* and *Yamato* were the biggest battleships ever built, at over 70,000 tons. They were also equipped with the biggest guns (46cm) and the heaviest armour. They were sunk (in October 1944 and April 1945 respectively) following massed attacks by US torpedo planes and dive bombers.

When the British *Dreadnought* was launched in 1906, every other battleship then afloat was outclassed. This revolutionary new capital ship was the first armed with 'all big guns', and had superior firepower and speed to all others. Within 40 years, such battleships would be obsolete because of their vulnerability to modern submarines. Carrier-aircraft assaults, such as the Japanese attack on Pearl Harbor in December 1941, sealed the battleship's doom. Nonetheless, two magnificent examples, America's *Iowa* Class super-dreadnoughts *Wisconsin* and *Missouri*, survived to play a role in the Gulf War of 1991, before being decommissioned to become museums.

HMS *LION*

Heavily-gunned but lightly-armoured, battle cruisers like the *Lion* were relatively fast, but often fatally vulnerable.

W. L. Wyllie

THE FIGUREHEAD

Even when not at war, submarines are still very dangerous ships to operate. Since one individual mistake could be disastrous for all, comradeship and excellence in performance are vital for safe and efficient operation. Thus submariners are fiercely proud of their ship and devoted to her well-being. One way of expressing this pride is through the ceremonial flag staff figurehead erected when the submarine is in harbour. The magnificent example shown was that of HMS *Poseidon* which unfortunately collided with a ship in 1931 killing twenty of her crew.

EAST AND WEST

Being island races dependent on the sea for trade, Britain and Japan have much in common and there was close co-operation for a short time between the two navies. For example the design of the Japanese *RO* Class submarine was based on the British *L* Class.

BIG GUNS

This submarine, HMS *M1* armed with a monster 12 inch gun was intended to pop up to the surface when the enemy was sighted, and then bombard him until the fleet battleships joined in. It was assumed that her low profile would keep her safe from retaliation. Fortunately the theory was never tested!

MINELAYING

The monitor submarine HMS *M3*, sister to the gun-armed *M1* and aircraft-equipped *M2*, was converted into a minelayer. She demonstrated that a submarine could be a truly effective minelaying platform because of the large number of mines she carried under her casing (upperworks), enabling her to sow her deadly cargo over a large area of the sea bed. She could also reach parts that were too dangerous for ships and aircraft.

THE MIGHTY FRENCH *SURCOUF*

Designed as a raider against merchant ships, this was the biggest and most famous submarine in the world in her day. She had everything; the greatest displacement; a range of 10,000 miles; two 8 inch guns; 22 torpedoes and a seaplane! In WWII this monster fought gallantly for the Allies, but was sunk by accident in 1942.

Submarines between the Wars

Britain's immediate reaction to the submarine at the end of WWI was an attempt to get it banned! Her allies did not agree, although a limit was put on the total number of submarines in each navy. A common conclusion reached by naval analysts was that the submarine could be a crucial weapon in any future conflict, but it needed to be more effective with increased range, better weapons and higher speeds. Designers met the challenge with a variety of submarine shapes and sizes, many of which were impracticable and often dangerous to the crews. In addition, every major maritime nation also built standard submarines. Germany, too, was making progress in the development of more powerful submarines. Hitler was not slow in instigating the means to produce high quality submarines quickly. This was something the Allies were going to discover to their cost.

RECREATION

Obviously there was not the room on board to enjoy much by way of recreation, so games such as draughts, dominoes, crib and 'uckers' (a submarine version of ludo) were dominant features of mess life. All these apparently innocent games were played with cut-throat intensity, and to be an individual champion on board provided a status that enhanced even the lowliest rank. A great treat and distraction would be the nightly film, even though the projector was forever running out of oil or breaking down!

ROVING EYES

The gun turret was replaced in HMS *M2* by a hanger and a small recoverable aircraft which was to act as 'eyes' to the fleet. This conversion recognised the part that aircraft would play in future maritime conflicts. It is sad that both *M1* and *M2* were lost in accidents.

FRESH FOOD!

Fresh food such as vegetables and fruit lasted for only a few days in a submarine before they went 'off'. The diet on board was dominated by meals that were either dehydrated or out of a can, and it was remarkable how many variations could be made out of spam! Extra rations of orange juice were supplied to maintain vitamin levels, and bread was baked overnight. But a banana, no matter how ancient, was always a treat!

DEWOITINE D.520

In 1939 the French Dewoitine company began making the D.520, generally considered the best French fighter of the Second World War. Its 910-horsepower engine was made by Hispano-Suiza, and it was specially arranged so that a big 20mm cannon could fit on top of the crankcase firing through the hub of the propeller. The D.520 also had two machine guns in each wing, and had a top speed of 530 km/h (329 mph).

BOEING F4B-1

The F4B family were US Navy counterparts of the Hawker Fury. They had another kind of engine in which the cylinders were arranged radially like the spokes of a wheel and covered in thin fins so that they could be cooled by air. The resulting aircraft looked much less streamlined, but in fact the air-cooled radial was usually lighter. As it was also shorter it made the fighter more manoeuvrable, and it did not need a heavy drag-producing water radiator.

THE CHANGING ENGINE

In the First World War many fighters had rotary engines such as the 130-horsepower Clerget (left). The entire engine rotated together with the propeller, and this acted like a top (a gyroscope) and made piloting difficult. After 1918 designers made static radials, such as the 450-horsepower Bristol Jupiter (right). Apart from having nine instead of seven cylinders, this differed in using ordinary petrol (gasoline) without lubricating oil having to be added.

Planes between the Wars

The First World War ended on 11 November 1918. For the next ten years there was little pressure to build better fighters, though engines developed dramatically. This development was further spurred by air racing. In 1931 a Rolls-Royce engine for racing developed 2,780 horsepower, though only for minutes at a time and using special fuels. Compared to the 130-horsepower engines on some fighters in the First World War, this was a huge leap and triggered the development of much better fuels for air force squadrons. Also, by 1930, a few designers were finding out how to make aircraft with a metal skin. The wire-braced biplanes of the past had fabric covering and these were replaced by all-metal 'stressed-skin' monoplanes. This so dramatically reduced drag that fighter speeds jumped from 322 km/h (200 mph) to over 563 km/h (350 mph). In turn this led to cockpits covered by transparent canopies, improved engine installations, flaps on the wings to slow the landing, and landing gears that could retract in flight. Some of these developments were opposed by fighter pilots, who could not believe that a fighter could be a sleek monoplane with an enclosed cockpit.

POLIKARPOV I-153

This Soviet biplane was unusual among biplanes in having retractable landing gear. The wheels folded directly backwards, at the same time rotating through 90 degrees so that they could lie flat in the underside of the aircraft. The I-153 had a radial engine, but it was enclosed in a neat cowling to reduce drag. Thus, this fighter could reach 430 km/h (267 mph), about 100 km/h (62 mph) faster than the Fury and F4B.

HAWKER FURIES

In the days before jet aircraft there were two basic kinds of engine. Some had their cylinders (usually 12) cooled by water and arranged in two lines. When installed in the aircraft they resulted in a long and pointed nose, as in these Fury fighters of the Royal Air Force (RAF) in 1932. This looked very streamlined, but in fact to cool the water such engines needed a big radiator and this slowed the aircraft down.

World War II (1939~45)

If the reasons surrounding the outbreak of World War I were complex and are, even now, unclear, the reasons for the outbreak of the Second World War are much easier to explain and grew directly out of unresolved issues at the end of the first world conflict. From a military point of view, many lessons had been learned from the First World War. In that war enemy troops still lined up in front of one another, in the time-honoured tradition, to 'shoot it out'. Battles in World War II were much more tactical and relied heavily on the increased use of technology and weapons of mass destruction. The war has been the bloodiest conflict in history thus far.

Altogether, some 40 million people lost their lives, including many civilians and 6 million Jews who were persecuted by the Germans and deliberately put to death in 'concentration camps'.

THE BLITZ

Having failed to defeat the British Air Force, Hitler continued his invasion plans by subjecting Britain to nightly bombing raids, both to destroy strategic targets and demoralise the civilian population. London was particularly badly hit as were other city centres throughout the world, including Dresden in Germany, bombed by the Allies.

GENERAL ROMMEL (1891-1944)

General Erwin Rommel was one of Hitler's leading generals in the early part of the war commanding Germany's highly successful tank corps. His defeat at El Alamein in north Africa, in 1942, is generally considered to be a turning point in the war.

AMERICA JOINS THE WAR

Japan joined forces with Germany and Italy, extending the war to much of Asia. Initially, America helped supply the allies against the Germans but was drawn directly into the conflict on 7 December 1941 when the Japanese launched an unprovoked attack on the U.S. fleet at Pearl Harbor, in Hawaii.

SUICIDE MISSIONS

Japanese soldiers had a reputation for fanaticism and would lay down their lives for their emperor rather than surrender or be shot. The 'kamikaze' pilots shown here were specially trained for suicide missions, to crash their planes, loaded with explosives, into the heart of the enemy. The word kamikaze means 'divine wind'.

D-DAY LANDINGS

The allies began their decisive push back against the Germans on 6 June 1944 with the re-invasion of France along the Normandy coast, known as 'Operation Overlord'. The Channel coast had been made impregnable by the Germans with a chain of fortifications. A British invention called 'Mulberries', or floating harbours, made the invasion possible. All told, some 5,000 ships transported over 300,000 men, 54,000 vehicles and 100,000 tons of supplies across the Channel, protected overhead by some 10,000 aeroplanes. Within a year the war in Europe was over (8 May 1945), followed 3 months later by the end of hostilities in south-east Asia.

BATTLE OF BRITAIN

In July 1940, shortly after France had fallen to the Germans, Hitler launched '*Operation Sealion*', the code-name for his intended invasion of Britain. For the invasion to succeed, however, Hitler needed to establish air supremacy, so he threw the full might of the German airforce, the Luftwaffe, against Britain. For over 2 months an aerial battle (the Battle of Britain) was fought out in the skies above South-East England. It was the first major battle in history to be fought solely in the air. Losses were heavy, but the British Spitfires and Hurricanes eventually won the day over the German Messerschmitt 109s (shown left), preventing the invasion.

Submarines in WWII

GERMAN COMMAND

Admiral Karl Doenitz assumed command of the U-boat force in 1935. He foresaw the forthcoming war with Britain and wanted 300 U-boats. Fortunately for the Allies he did not get them. He made the best of what he had though by concentrating them in wolf-packs, and succeeded in sinking hundreds of merchant vessels.

Whilst Hitler and his Nazis were determined to overrun continental Europe, they wanted nothing from Britain but to be left alone. Indeed they were convinced that if they allowed 'Britannia to rule the waves', they could avoid a general conflict. Thus Germany maintained only a small navy, whereas her army and air force were built up significantly for the invasions ahead. When war with Britain did break out, the Germans soon realised that naval engagements in the classical sense were out of the question, and only by attacking commerce could they make their presence felt at sea. The early years of the Battle of the Atlantic, despite convoys and ASDIC fitted escorts, saw the success of the U-boats. But not for long.

DEADLY CARGO

The deadly cargo of torpedoes can be seen in this Type VIIb U-boat. A total of twelve would be carried, and the Commanding Officer would endeavour to make every weapon count by getting in close to the target, crippling it with one torpedo, and finishing it off with his gun. The invention of radar and the introduction of long range Coastal Command aircraft swung the battle against the U-boat. By the end of the war, over 750 U-boats were destroyed with huge loss of life.

U-BOAT PEN

A tug boat is guiding the Japanese submarine I29 into the safety of a German re-inforced concrete, bomb proof U-boat pen in Bordeaux, France. Japanese submarines made a number of very long distance trips to collect secret equipment from their German allies.

THE COCKLESHELL HEROES

An important task for British submarines was landing and recovering agents and special forces. One of the most famous exploits was the Special Boat Service's highly successful raid on Bordeaux when they sank several ships with limpet mines. Their 'cockles' were launched from HMS *Tuna*. Ten extremely brave Royal Marines took part in the operation; eight were killed.

THE KNIGHT'S CROSS

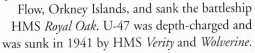

This was a German medal awarded for extreme bravery. An early winner in U-boats was Gunter Prien, the captain of *U-47*. In October 1939 he pulled off one of the most spectacular exploits of the war when he penetrated British defences at Scapa Flow, Orkney Islands, and sank the battleship HMS *Royal Oak*. U-47 was depth-charged and was sunk in 1941 by HMS *Verity* and *Wolverine*.

U-47'S BRIDGE

Until 1944 (when some boats were fitted with the 'Schnorkel') U-boats had to surface for transit to their patrol areas. During transit they were at high risk of attack from the air, so the bridge would be crowded with lookouts and anti-aircraft gunners!

JAPANESE SUBMARINES

Despite having the best torpedo in the world (the Long Lance), Japanese submarines were never allowed to make an effective contribution to the overall Battle of the Pacific. They were not used as an independent offensive arm. Instead they were fleet escorts, as they had been in World War I, and the Japanese Navy wasted their energies by building huge submarines capable of little else than being communication ships, or tankers for flying boats.

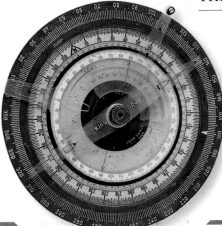

LONG DISTANCE TRAVEL

U-boats were employed to attack merchant ships, so they had to travel long distances to intercept Allied convoys sailing across the Atlantic. The convoys sailed as far north as possible to try to escape detection. This made the U-boats' job difficult, but their range of 6,500 miles meant that their prey was always within reach.

THE TORPEDO CALCULATOR

Achieving a torpedo hit against a moving target was a complicated business. The most important factor was knowing when to fire so that the weapon intercepted the target track at the right moment. Adding torpedo angles and fans to cover range, aspect and speed inaccuracies often made it too difficult for the Captain to calculate without help.

AN AWARD FOR MALTA

Malta was crucial to the conduct of the campaign against Rommel's Afrika Corps. It was home to Royal Air Force bomber and fighter aircraft and the *Fighting Tenth* submarine squadron. Despite being pulverised by German bombers both by day and night, the starving islanders resolutely refused to surrender. In recognition of their supreme courage, King George VI bestowed on them the highest civilian award for bravery, The George Cross.

HANGING ON

It took luck to survive a submarine attack. Often there was no time to launch lifeboats, and men would cling onto any wreckage that floated, without food and water and for days on end. They were the unsung heroes of the war.

A HOMECOMING CELEBRATION

This cake was baked by the mother of telegraphist Albert Hamilton-Smith to celebrate his return home. Tragically his submarine, HMS *P33*, was lost with all hands off Tripoli in August 1941. The cake was kept in his memory.

TORPEDOES AWAY!

This torpedo space of a large Japanese submarine contained six tubes. At the wet end of the tubes were the bow caps, which would be opened as the submarine prepared to launch. When the Captain ordered 'Fire', high pressure air expelled the weapons. When the torpedoes moved, triggers in the tubes would start their engines. Thereafter they were on their own, following predetermined calculated courses towards their target.

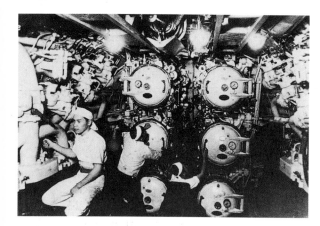

INFERIOR MACHINES

Italian submarines operated in the North Atlantic under the command of Admiral Doenitz. They were technically inferior to his U-boats and he was so disappointed with their performance that he moved over 60 of his own precious submarines into the Mediterranean to counter the British fleet. This in turn weakened his campaign against Allied merchant shipping.

THE *REGIA MARINA*

This Italian submarine surrendered in September 1943. Italy entered the war with 100 submarines, but at the time of her surrender 86 of them had been sunk or captured.

Submarines in World War II contd.

As well as in the North Atlantic, submarines also played an important, often vital, role in other areas of the war. In the Mediterranean, British submarines operating from Malta and Alexandria fought a desperate battle against General Rommel's supply lines to North Africa. In conjunction with the Royal Air Force they deprived Rommel of half of what he needed by way of reinforcements, and stopped him reaching the Suez Canal. In the Far East the Japanese, having conquered all the western islands of the Pacific, found themselves subjected to an onslaught by the United States Submarine Service against which they had little effective defence. British submarines were also active with the Americans from the Allied base in Fremantle, Western Australia. Although losses were much less than those of Germany, nevertheless a significant proportion of allied submariners (including French, Dutch, Polish, Russian and Greek) lost their lives, many of them to the deadliest of WWII anti-submarine weapons... the mine.

A PRESENT FROM MOIRA

Every Royal Navy submarine had a 'trophy' which was closely related to its name. For example HMS *Tallyho* had a hunting horn, HMS *Turpin* had a flintlock pistol and HMS *Totem* had a totem pole. HMS *Tiptoe* not only had a ballet dancer on her badge, but also boasted a pair of ballet shoes presented by the famous ballerina, Moira Shearer. Miss Shearer had worn them during the making of the film 'The Red Shoes'. HMS *Tiptoe* had the distinction of being the last submarine to sink an enemy ship in WWII by torpedo when in August 1945, she sent a Japanese freighter to the bottom of the Pacific.

THE SUBMARINE GUN

Being small, Italian submarines could carry more shells for the gun than torpedoes, so it was an ideal weapon house against lightly armed opposition which didn't have aircraft cover.

AN EXCEPTIONAL VOLUNTEER

The tankard belonged to HMS *Storm*, the only submarine ever to have been commanded by an officer in the Royal Navy Volunteer Reserve. The RNVR were men and women who were not in a maritime profession at the outbreak of war, so to be given command of a submarine meant that you were an exceptional individual. The man concerned was Lieutenant Commander Edward Young DSO DSC RNVR.

UNIFORM OF A CHARIOTEER

In the early days equipment used by the crew of the 'Chariots' was crude and dangerous, and was simply a conversion of submarine escape equipment, ill-suited to the rigours of physical exertion. Eventually specialist equipment, such as this helmet, was developed and they emerged looking like the modern frogman.

ROOM FOR TWO

'Chariots' had a crew of two. It was the Number 1's job to navigate and control the craft; the Number 2 cleared away obstructions and placed the explosive charge against the target. This charge was in fact the chariot's detachable nose.

THE ITALIAN HUMAN TORPEDO

The Italians were the great pioneers of the midget submarine and had built their first prototype in 1935. Their outstandingly brave team of volunteers achieved one of the most astonishing feats of World War II.
In December 1941, three human torpedoes sank the battleships HMS *Queen Elizabeth* and *Valiant* in Alexandria Harbour in Egypt. This could have changed the course of the war. However the water was shallow, so both ships settled on the bottom with their upper part still intact, which allowed them to simulate readiness for sea by emitting funnel smoke. Because the Italian crews had been captured, the Italian High Command never realised how close they were to naval dominance of the Mediterranean.

SMALL BUT DEADLY

It was the British who produced the most effective midget submarine of the war; the four man, diesel-electric powered 'X-craft'. Introduced in 1943, their armament consisted of two large side cargoes of high explosive, releasable from inside the submarine, which were designed to be laid under the target.
Four Victoria Crosses, the highest award for gallantry, were awarded to crews who successfully crippled the German battleship *Tirpitz* in a Norwegian fjord, and the Japanese cruiser *Takao* in Singapore Harbour.

THE JAPANESE *HA*-BOAT

Along with 27 large submarines, five torpedo armed Japanese *HA*-boats took part in the raid on Pearl Harbor in December 1941. Their task was to infiltrate the harbour and sink the stationary American battle-fleet. None succeeded, and all five were destroyed. The Japanese Navy pinned great hopes on this type of submarine and built them in vast quantities. In fact few opportunities for their use ever emerged, and they proved an expensive distraction.

Midget Submarines

The only way to sink ships berthed in harbours or anchorages that were too shallow or too well defended to allow attack by full sized submarines, was through the use of Midget Submarines. There were three main types. The human torpedo, first developed by the Italians and known as the 'chariot' in British circles, which fixed a detachable warhead to its target; the British 'X' craft, a perfect submarine in miniature with detachable explosive charges; and the two man, torpedo firing, submersible developed by the Japanese and Germans. All Midget submarines had a limited range and had to be transported to their target area by a mother submarine, which would then await their return. In fact very few crews were ever recovered. They knew that many were setting out on a one way mission, the end result of which would be capture....or death.

SUCH LITTLE SPACE

Space inside this miniature submarine was so cramped that there was only room for one of the four crew to stretch out and sleep. Food was cooked over a tiny Bunsen burner stove, and there was a primitive toilet. This lock-in/lock-out compartment allowed the diver to leave the submarine to clear obstructions and plant limpet mines if required.

THE AMERICAN X-2

Not to be left out of the miniature arms race, the US Navy began experimenting with different designs. One such experiment was with this Fairchild-built torpedo firing Midget submarine. However, whilst these tests were being carried out, bigger submarines had done the job already.

MOBILE MIDGETS

The introduction of the German midget submarine 'Bibel' was an attempt to stave off the Allied invasion of Europe. A miniature U-boat fleet of about 390 craft was built. All of the designs had an underslung torpedo, and were highly mobile. Like the Japanese, German strategists misused their midget submarines by attempting to employ them in orthodox submarine roles. Their true, and only, strength was against a static and landlocked target.

FAMOUS FIGHTERS

Whereas the Allies in the Second World War used dozens of different fighters, the German Luftwaffe relied on 33,000 Bf 109s, later joined by 20,000 Fw 190s. The Messerschmitt Bf 109 (in the distance) was first flown in April 1935, but by fitting more powerful engines and heavier armament it was kept formidable to the end of the War. Some Bf 109 pilots managed to shoot down over 300 enemy aircraft. The Spitfire (in the foreground) was the most successful Allied fighter and also the most famous. A later and more advanced design than the Hurricane, the Spitfire was developed through 24 versions, starting in 1938 weighing 2,495 kg (5,500 lb) and a speed of 583 km/h (362 mph) and ending in 1945 weighing (5,269 kg (11,615 lb) and with a speed almost 160 km/h (100 mph) greater!

HAWKER HURRICANE

Compared with the Bf 109 the British Hurricane was rather more primitive in design, being larger and, until 1941, covered in fabric like a fighter of the First World War. Major advantages of the Hurricane were that it was easy to fly, very tough and easy to repair. In the Battle of Britain, Hurricanes shot down more German aircraft than everything else combined.

AFTER THE BATTLE

By the end of the War towns and villages throughout Europe bore the scars of air attack. This town in Normandy (northern France) was actually fought over in 1944. Just outside would have been the RAF fighters, based on a hurriedly constructed airfield with the pilots living in tents. The runway would be a bulldozed field with a long strip of steel mesh laid down to give a smooth surface.

LEADERS OF THE LUFTWAFFE

In 1933 the German air force, forbidden after 1918, was reborn as The Luftwaffe. The Commander was Field Marshal Hermann Goering, who was to become a significant Nazi leader over the War period, and he appointed Ernst Udet (right) to choose the planes. Both men were fighter aces in the First World War.

Planes in WWII: Europe

The Second World War (1939–45) firmly established the military role of aeroplanes. The Battle of Britain, which in the summer and autumn of 1940 certainly changed the entire course of history, was the first time since 1918 that large numbers of fighters had engaged in deadly air combat. This time, virtually all the fighters were streamlined stressed-skin monoplanes, with engines of over 1,000 horsepower and maximum speeds significantly higher than 480 km/h (300 mph). The combined Allied air forces in Britain were outnumbered by the German Luftwaffe (air force), and also had the disadvantage that Britain's airfields had been heavily bombed. However, the British had one huge advantage – the invention of radar. Instead of fighters flying aimlessly waiting for an enemy encounter, every Luftwaffe attack was plotted and pilots were given accurate directions for interception.

WAAF PLOTTERS

In the Second World War more than one-third of the duties on the ground in the RAF were done by members of the Women's Auxiliary Air Force. One of their jobs was to keep track of the great air battles over Britain and North-West Europe by moving special symbols over huge maps.

SPITFIRE PILOTS

The Second World War began in September 1939, and by the end of 1940 the RAF had lost more pilots than it had at the start. It was thus extremely important that hundreds of pilots found their way to England from the countries overrun by Germany, such as Poland, Czechoslovakia, France, Belgium, the Netherlands, Denmark and Norway. Many others came from Commonwealth countries such as Canada, Australia, South Africa and New Zealand. Without them Britain's situation would have been even more serious.

Planes in WWII: Pacific

PEARL HARBOR

The Imperial Navy used three main types in their carefully planned surprise attack: the 'Zero' fighter, the Aichi D3A dive bomber and the Nakajima B5N torpedo bomber. All were quite ordinary aircraft, but their combined attack proved devastating. For the US Navy there was only one bit of good fortune: their vital aircraft carriers were away at sea, and so survived. Later, it was to be the aircraft from those carriers that were to destroy the mighty Japanese fleet.

On 7 December 1941 the Japanese Imperial Navy Air Force attacked the US Pacific Fleet at Pearl Harbor, in Hawaii. This act brought both countries into the War. At that time almost nothing was known about Japanese aircraft, the Allies having the idea that they were all flimsy inferior copies of American and British designs. Nothing could have been further from the truth! One fighter alone, the Navy Mitsubishi A6M2, commonly known as the Zero, shot down with ease every Allied aircraft it encountered. This was surprising as it had an engine of only just over 1,000 horsepower. After this shock, Japanese aircraft were taken very seriously. By 1944 many Japanese were flying Kamikaze suicide missions, deliberately crashing their bomb-laden aircraft on to Allied ships. Fighters found it difficult to defend against such attacks. Towards the end of the War, the Japanese best was the Nakajima Ki-84 Hayate (Gale). Gradually such aircraft as the US Navy F6F and F4U gained the upper hand.

KAMIKAZE PILOTS

In the final year of the War thousands of Japanese chose to undertake many kinds of suicide mission. These pilots had volunteered for Kamikaze missions.

The Kamikaze was a great wind which hundreds of years earlier had scattered an enemy fleet. In October 1944 Japanese pilots first decided to load up their aircraft with explosives and crash them on enemy ships in the Philippines, and later at Okinawa. By 1944 the Imperial Navy even had tiny rocket aircraft, so fast they were almost impossible to shoot down, with the whole nose filled with explosives.

ADVERSARIES
IN THE SKY

Apart from the Imperial Army's Kawasaki Ki-61, all the mass-produced Japanese fighters had air-cooled radial engines. By 1943 these engines had been developed to over 1,900 horsepower, and this made possible even more formidable fighters. By this time such US Navy fighters as the F6F Hellcat (right, taking off from an aircraft carrier) and F4U Corsair had achieved supremacy over the 'Zero' and other 1,000-horsepower types, but the Imperial Army's Nakajima Ki-84 (left) was typical of the new species. Though it did not quite reach 644 km/h (400 mph), the Ki-84 was a brilliant all-round aircraft. However, most of the Japanese pilots were inexperienced, and they never again got the upper hand.

A JAPANESE ZERO

The Zero only had just over 1,000 horsepower, but it was so light it could outfly its opponents, and then destroy them with its two 20mm cannon.

ENOLA GAY

In great secrecy the USA, assisted by British scientists, had invented atomic bombs, one of which could destroy a city. On 6 August this B-29, named 'Enola Gay' after the aircraft commander's wife, dropped such a bomb on Hiroshima. Three days later another, named 'Bock's Car', dropped a different kind of bomb on Nagasaki. The Japanese surrendered.

BRISTOL BEAUFIGHTER

The Beaufighter was a massive, powerful and tough long-range fighter with devastating armament of four cannon and six machine guns. Once it was equipped with radar it proved ideal as a night fighter, entering RAF service in this role in late 1940.

Night Fighters

A few aircraft in the First World War were intended for fighting at night, especially against airships, but the technology for such a task did not exist. By the Second World War it was commonplace for aircraft to fly at night, but it was still almost impossible to hunt down enemy aircraft on a dark night. The breakthrough was the development of radar sets small enough to be carried inside aircraft. Such AI (Airborne Interception) radar comprises boxes of electronics and various antennae. These aim an electronic beam into the sky ahead, while other antennas pick up reflections from enemy aircraft. Primitive AI in 1940 was bulky and heavy, and needed skilled operators. Thus, the AI-equipped fighter had to be large and powerful. The first successful type was the Bristol Beaufighter, used in the War to shoot down Luftwaffe bombers, and later to fire torpedoes and rockets against enemy ships. In 1942 came the de Havilland Mosquito. Faster than the 'Beau', this brilliant aircraft served as a bomber, a day and night fighter and attack aircraft, a long-range reconnaissance aircraft and even for goods transport. Soon the Luftwaffe was fitting radars into their aircraft, and from 1943 they also added a new kind of armament installation, in the form of powerful cannon firing at a steep angle upwards. This meant they could attack from underneath and Allied planes literally never knew what hit them.

MOSQUITO COCKPIT

The de Havilland Mosquito was even better than the Beaufighter. Though it was made of wood, it was one of the fastest aircraft in the sky, and it could fly almost any kind of mission. The pilot sat on the left in a rather 'cosy' cockpit, with the navigator on his right, just far enough back for elbows not to clash. Here the pilot's controls of a Mk XII night fighter are on the left, beyond the top of his control column, with its gun-firing button. On the right are the radar displays and controls, managed by the navigator.

LUFTWAFFE NIGHT FIGHTER

First flown in May 1936, the Messerschmitt Bf 110 was planned as a formidable twin-engined, long-range fighter to escort the Luftwaffe bombers. In the Battle of Britain they proved easy targets for Hurricanes and Spitfires, but were about to become very useful. Fitted with more powerful DB 605 engines, and with a crew of three, they were packed with radar in order to find RAF bombers at night. This late-1944 Bf 110G-4B/U1 has a mass of radar antennae on the nose, as well as special exhausts which showed no visible flames at night.

THE BEST NIGHT FIGHTER PILOT

Major Heinz Wolfgang Schnaufer shot down an amazing 121 RAF heavy bombers at night. He survived the War, only to be killed soon afterwards in a traffic accident.

SCHRÄGE MUSIK

This is German for 'slanting music', or jazz. It was their code-name for a special kind of armament for night fighters. Two or more heavy cannon would be installed in the middle of the fighter, pointing steeply upwards at 70 to 80 degrees. Skilled pilots would find an RAF heavy bomber and, carefully formating underneath it, would aim the guns at the spars of the wing. A quick burst, and the bomber would lose a wing. Provided the fighter got out of the way of the falling bomber there was no danger, because the RAF bombers were totally 'blind' underneath.

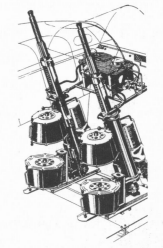

BLACK WIDOW

In the USA Northrop created one of the first aircraft ever planned as a night fighter from the outset. This big machine had a bulging central nacelle packed with radar, guns and a crew of three. The tail was carried on two booms. Fully loaded the P-61 Black Widow weighed up to 15 tons.

The First Jets

Towards the end of the Second World War, the engines of the latest war planes were cumbersome masses of metal weighing over a ton, yet with every part made like a fine Swiss watch. Even though the latest fighters had become heavier, the massive engines could propel them at over 724 km/h (450 mph). The difficulty was that it was almost impossible to make traditional fighters go any faster. Even more serious was the fact that ordinary propellers were reaching a fundamental speed limit. Thus the fighters of 1944-45 were the end of an era. In both Britain and Germany the turbojet engine was being developed. Frank Whittle had invented the first turbojet engine in Britain in 1929 but nobody was interested. Six years later in Germany, Hans von Ohain thought of the same idea, and the first jet aircraft flew in Germany in August 1939.

Nothing much happened to Whittle's engine until one was sent to the USA. Then things moved fast, and the first Allied jet fighter, the American Bell P-59 Airacomet, flew on 2 October 1942. However, the much greater German effort resulted in a shoal of jet aircraft. The most important was the Messerschmitt Me 262, and had the Germans not been defeated in 1945 their jets would have been a big problem for the Allies.

A NEW BREED OF PILOT

R.P. 'Bee' Beamont was a fighter pilot throughout the War, and afterwards he became even more famous in Britain as a test pilot. He tested Hawker Typhoons and Tempests, followed by Gloster Meteor jets and many other types, before becoming Chief Test Pilot on the Canberra jet bomber, Lightning, TSR.2, Jaguar and Tornado.

ROCKET INTERCEPTOR

The Messerschmitt Me 163B was a strange tailless rocket interceptor with the pilot in the nose along with two 30mm cannon. Behind him were tons of deadly liquids which fed a rocket engine in the tail. It was a tricky 'last-ditch' weapon which killed many of its own pilots,

GLOSTER METEOR

First of the British jets, the Gloster Meteor had two Whittle-type engines, and first flew in March 1943. This was one of the prototypes, as indicated by the big 'P' in a circle. After the War a later version set a speed record at over 975 km/h (616 mph).

MESSERSCHMITT Me 262A-1A

The Me 262 was a superb all-round fighter and fighter-bomber powered by two Jumo 004B turbojets slung under the wings. In the nose was the formidable armament of four 30mm cannon. With a speed of 845 km/h (525 mph), it was much faster than any Allied aircraft. The Me 262 would have been even more of a problem to the Allies had not Adolf Hitler misguidedly decreed that they all be used as bombers.

LAVOCHKIN La-7

At the end of the Second World War the Russians had no jet aircraft, and typical of their fighters was the La-7, powered by a 2,000-horsepower piston engine. For the desperately harsh conditions on the Russian front aircraft had to be very tough and simple. The La-7 was nevertheless at least equal to fighters from any other country.

SIR FRANK WHITTLE

As a young and very junior RAF pilot in 1929 Frank Whittle invented the turbojet. He proved mathematically that it could work, but his superiors in the Air Ministry were not interested. At his own expense he took out a patent, finally granted in January 1930, but still nobody showed the slightest interest. At last, in desperation, he and a group of friends found just enough money actually to build a turbojet, which he started up on 12 April 1937. This amazed the officials and experts, but by this time hundreds of engineers were working on jets in Germany, and their's was the first jet aircraft to fly.

RECOGNITION BOOK

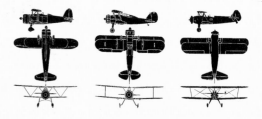

To the inexperienced eye, all aircraft (with some exceptions) look quite similar. Recognition manuals became standard issue for fighter pilots although many never became skilled at telling friend from foe. This page from a 1941 recognition book shows (from the left): a Fiat C.R.42, an Italian fighter; a Gloster Gladiator, a British fighter; and a Boeing (Stearman) PT-13, an American trainer.

THE SECOND WORLD WAR

This pilot (right) is wearing standard British flying clothing. The one-piece overall was pulled on from below and fastened with zips. In the front of the legs are pockets for maps and other documents (though pilots had to be very careful what they took with them over enemy territory). Most operational clothing could be plugged in and electrically heated. He is actually wearing his oxygen mask, so with goggles in place no part of his face is visible. His kit is completed by long cape-leather gloves and sheepskin-lined boots, and his seat-type parachute is on the ground.

PARATROOPS

This Italian magazine of about 1940 is making propaganda out of Italy's parachute troops, which used to descend from the sky to capture enemy targets. Such a means of attack was pioneered in the Soviet Union, and then adopted on a large scale by the Germans. Thousands of paratroops were used in Belgium in 1940 and to capture Crete in 1941. Even larger numbers were used by the British and Americans in 1944-5

PARACHUTE PACKS

In the 1920s it gradually became universal for fighter pilots to wear parachutes. This Belgian pilot is wearing a British Irvin type of pilot parachute, with the canopy and shroud lines all tightly folded inside a pack which formed a cushion on which the pilot sat. The fighter's seat was an aluminium 'bucket' type with a big hollow in which the parachute fitted. He wears a leather helmet, goggles (because he had an open cockpit) and cavalry type boots.

Fighter Pilots of World War II

It seems astonishing today that the fighter pilots of the First World War did not have parachutes and were not even strapped in to their cockpits. One of the greatest British aces, Major Albert Ball VC, was found one day lying dead on the ground. There was no aircraft near, and no German claimed to have shot him down, and it was thought he must have simply fallen out of his fighter. By the mid-1930s the fighter pilot climbed into his cockpit, sat on his parachute, strapped tightly into his seat, and then had to plug in both his radio cable and oxygen pipe. Training programmes were also developed. Pilots would learn on simple primary trainers, and after as little as 40 hours, they would progress to more powerful trainers, such as the T-6 Texan (or Harvard). At something over 150 hours they would progress to operational fighters and would practise firing at targets towed on a long cable by special tug aircraft. By 1942 pilots were learning to drop bombs and fire rockets, both challenging tasks as the weapons had no inbuilt guidance as they do today.

MUSTANG PILOT

In the Second World War one of the best Allied fighters was the North American P-51 Mustang. This pilot would have much in common with pilots of the past, but much more equipment. His helmet would be fitted with headphones, and on the front it carried an oxygen mask (note the big pipe going to it) and integral microphone.

WASPS

In the USA there were so many women pilots that many of them were organized into the Women's Auxiliary Service Pilots to ferry all kinds of aircraft from factory to squadron, and often to repair or modification centres.

Weapons & Warfare Since WWII

Since the end of hostilities in the Second World War there have been well over 100 major conflicts in some 70 countries world-wide. Many of these have been localised disputes, in under developed regions of the world, but several have been potentially inflammatory and may have led to further world-wide conflicts and have had to be quickly resolved. Following the end of the Second World War an arms race began between America (and her allies) and the Soviet Union. Each side acquired sufficient nuclear weapons to destroy the world several times over. Arms agreements were eventually reached in the 1980s and 90s and many warheads were disarmed, but since then several other countries have acquired weapons of mass destruction putting the world under constant threat of nuclear attack. Another feature of modern warfare has been the development of germ-warfare, where warheads containing lethal cocktails of bacteria are released on an unsuspecting civilian population.

KOREAN WAR

In 1910 Korea was annexed by Japan. When Japan surrendered at the end of World War II Russian troops occupied North Korea and American troops occupied the south of the country.
In 1950 the Communist North Koreans, backed by the Soviets, invaded South Korea, which was aided by America and Britain, resulting in civil war. Open hostilities ended in 1953, but all attempts to unite the two factions have failed and they remain separate countries.

GUIDED MISSILES

The idea of exploding rockets was first used by the Chinese as early as 1232. The first guided missile was launched in 1917, an automatically piloted biplane called 'Bug' SSM. During World War II, German scientists perfected the V1 and V2 pilotless 'flying bombs'. Once launched, the engines were timed to run for a set period of time, before they fell and exploded on impact. Modern computer technology means that missiles can select a target with pin-point accuracy.

GULF WAR

On 2 August 1990 Saddam Hussein, President of Iraq, invaded neighbouring Kuwait in a dispute over oil prices. The United Nations imposed economic sanctions on Iraq and on 29 November issued a resolution authorising the use of military force to liberate Kuwait. Hussein had been stockpiling weapons and many feared a long, protracted war, but what followed was a brief, high-technology war resulting in an allied victory, headed by America and Britain. In 2003, an Allied force invaded Iraq again following fears that Saddam Hussein was stockpiling weapons of mass destruction. Hussein was captured and was put on trial for crimes against humanity.

A NEW FORCE

Modern military forces are better equipped with weapons of destruction than any of their predecessors. Weapons of devastating capability can be launched from vast distances. Although 'Smart' weapons can avoid hitting unnecessary targets, modern neutron bombs are now capable of emitting short-wave radiation that affect people but leave buildings still standing.

ATOMIC POWER

The scientists who developed the atomic bombs that were dropped on Japan, so bringing World War II to a close, were Germans who had fled the Nazi regime and found sanctuary in America. The first generation of atom bombs used a combination of conventional explosives to drive together elements of Uranium 235 to produce a chain reaction among the neutrons. From these developed hydrogen bombs, which were more powerful than atomic bombs. Nowadays, a whole range of devastatingly powerful nuclear weapons is available to add to the armouries of military powers. When Japan continued to fight, even after the surrender of Germany, drastic action was necessary. It was decided to drop two atomic bombs on Japanese cities, Hiroshima and Nagasaki (bottom right). So devastating were they that both cities were virtually razed to the ground and people still suffer the effects of radiation. Japan surrendered almost immediately, on 14 August 1939. The picture above shows a nuclear bomb test in the Bikini Atoll (in the Pacific) in 1954, with the typical mushroom-shaped cloud.

VIETNAM WAR

Civil war broke out in Vietnam in 1954 between the Communist-backed North and the American-backed South. The North used guerrilla warfare, using the jungle as a refuge. The Americans responded with a scorched-earth policy of deforestation, but it proved ineffective. American troops were gradually withdrawn between 1969–73 in response to public pressure. Two years later South Vietnam surrendered to communist rule.

Nuclear Submarines

*T*he defeat of Germany and her allies should have heralded peace and stability for the world. However, the late 1940s saw the start of the Cold War between the Eastern bloc communist countries and the Western democracies. Each side was trying to better the other by staying one step ahead in an arms race. Because of the increasing number of forces, the only way that the West, through the North Atlantic Treaty Organisation (NATO), could maintain a global balance of power was by technological superiority. One example of this was the development of the nuclear powered submarine, USS *Nautilus*, which made its first voyage in 1955. A new era of submarine dominance had dawned.

Military submarines are coded to show the type of weapons they carry such as nuclear-powered attack submarines (SSN) and nuclear-powered submarines carrying ballistic missiles (SSBN).

BREAKING THE ICE

A submarine's nuclear reactor makes it completely independent of the surface. This allows it to travel to many areas denied to diesel-electric submarines, such as the North Pole. The picture above shows USS *Trepang*, an attack submarine (SSN), having punched her way through the ice cap.

SURVEILLANCE

As HMS *Conqueror* demonstrated during the Falklands War in 1982, it is possible for any nuclear powered submarine to operate unsupported many thousands of miles from base. The only limiting factor for endurance is the amount of food she can carry. This periscope camera panoramic sweep shows the SSN's capability to conduct surveillance operations of a potential enemy's coastline.

KEEPING THE CREW HAPPY

Since crews of nuclear powered submarines spend many months on patrol, out of touch with their families, great effort is made to look after their morale. Food is an important factor, and catering is therefore of the highest quality. Expert cooks ensure that there is always a meal available. When the modern submariner is not on watch helping with the routine operation of the submarine, or completing the inevitable paperwork, he will relax by listening to music or watching movies, of which there is always a plentiful supply.

HIDE AND SEEK

Britain's first Polaris missile equipped SSBN, HMS *Resolution*, is shown on passage down the River Clyde heading for her patrol area. Her main aim on patrol would be to remain hidden.

Submarines: Attack & Defen[c]

Slowly but surely the idea of the submarine as a defensive weapon changed, and it became seen as the perfect platform to deliver a mighty blow under a cloak of stealth and surprise. So hulls became bigger and weapons more powerful. Short range torpedoes of half a mile gave way to the modern torpedo with a range of more than fifteen miles. The sea-skimming anti-ship missile, which can travel about seventy miles, has replaced the deck gun. A land attack is possible with the development of the *Tomahawk* tactical cruise missile (range 2,000 miles plus), which complements the huge strategic ballistic missiles such as *Trident*. Defensively the submarine has come a long way too - today it is fast, quiet, deep diving, very hard to detect, and can stay underwater for months.

LOW LEVEL MISSILES

An excellent anti-ship missile is the Sub-Harpoon which is fitted to all United States Navy and Royal Navy attack submarines, and seen here emerging from its launch capsule. It has a range in excess of seventy miles, and homes in on its target through the radar set in its nose. It skims the sea and approaches its target at very low level. It is therefore very difficult to detect and shoot down.

MAKING WEAPONS

The first torpedo factory in the world was in Fiume, Austria, where Sir Robert Whitehead, the torpedo pioneer, worked for the government. The modern equivalent of these late 19th century workers who, in their turn, were working at the forefront of technology, would be dressed in white, dustproof, anti-static coveralls and surrounded by computer wizardry!

THE INTER-CONTINENTAL BALLISTIC MISSILE

The purpose of these missiles is to deter aggression by a potential enemy who may be tempted to strike the first blow with weapons of mass destruction. In order for deterrence to work, retaliation against an aggressor must be effective and guaranteed. The submarine is an excellent platform on which to deploy these 'last resort' weapons since its position can be kept secret until the last moment. It can stay on the move, and can remain at sea for extended periods. When fired, missile warheads leave the earth's atmosphere for a short time before plunging onto their target making them almost impossible to defend against.

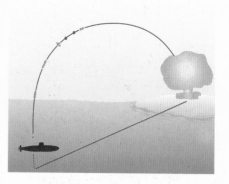

TORPEDO ATTACK

This picture shows the devastating effect of a torpedo against a large frigate. Modern torpedoes are fitted with a number of fuses (i.e. initiating devices). In this case it was the magnetic fuse that reacted, causing the torpedo to explode beneath the target. This created a vortex (hole) in the sea, and with the keel of the target ship unsupported, its back was broken. The other major type of fuse is impact, designed to set off the torpedo explosive when it physically strikes its target.

A SUBMARINE'S EARS

Just as the periscopes are the 'eyes' of the submarine, so its sonar sets are its 'ears'. Operators man the sets, and they are trained to listen for and recognise the many different sounds that fill the oceans.

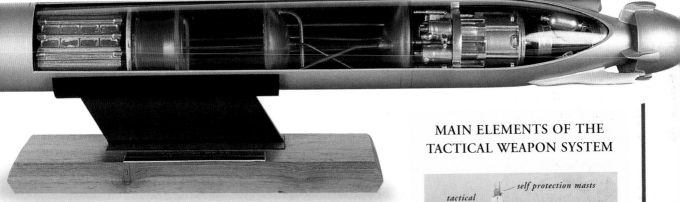

TACTICAL WEAPONS

The modern torpedo is an awesome weapon which, unlike the missile, will quickly sink the target it strikes. The firing submarine guides it by wire to the vicinity of the target, and when it is close enough, the torpedo will tell its guider that it is in contact. It will then home in on its target and attack giving the target little time to take avoiding action.

MAIN ELEMENTS OF THE TACTICAL WEAPON SYSTEM

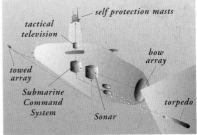

self protection masts
tactical television
towed array
bow array
Submarine Command System
Sonar
torpedo

The total weapon system enables a submarine to detect, classify, approach, and fire at its target. Detection will be achieved on sonar, and classification will be made by recognising the 'fingerprint' of the target. Because submarines try only to listen rather than transmit the traditional sonar 'ping' (which would give its presence away), it has to work very hard to determine when the target is within range of its torpedoes. Once the Captain is happy that he has a satisfactory solution, he will launch his weapon, giving his prey the minimum time to react.

SUBMARINE HUNTERS

A submarine is very agile, and a hunter can never be sure where it will pop up next. One of the most effective submarine hunters, apart from another submarine, is a helicopter. A pilot can watch over a large area of sea. Ships are usually not fast enough to pursue a fleeing submarine. A good strategy for hunting a submarine is to send other submarines out in pairs, carrying lightweight torpedoes to pack quite a punch.

Cold War Submarines

The Soviet Union exploded her first nuclear bomb in 1949, and within a year of USS *Nautilus* going to sea, she introduced her first operational nuclear powered submarine. Thus in the late 1950s the temperature of the Cold War was distinctly frosty, and the balance of military power lay with the Soviet dominated Warsaw Pact. A correction was needed by the West, and this arrived in 1960 with the launch of a Polaris ballistic missile by USS *George Washington*. This event had a huge political and military impact, since for the first time it was possible to attack enemy lands from a submerged submarine secure from discovery or attack. The world, whilst being a safer place in which to live, had changed forever.

INTERCONTINENTAL CO-OPERATION

Britain's first nuclear powered submarine, HMS *Dreadnought*, was launched in 1960. The decision for the Royal Navy to enter the nuclear age was taken by Earl Mountbatten, the First Sea Lord. It was a decision greatly welcomed by the United States, who provided *Dreadnought* with her nuclear reactor to help get her to sea as soon as possible. Since then the two navies have worked very closely together, with Britain adopting similar weapon systems and strategies to that of her more powerful ally. HMS *Vanguard*, a Trident missile submarine, is a current example of that co-operation.

THE NUCLEAR REACTOR

The process of nuclear fission that takes place inside a nuclear reactor produces a vast amount of heat, which boils water into steam. This then drives two main engines for propulsion and two turbo-generators for electrical power.

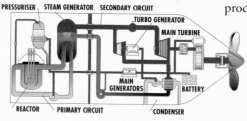

EVER READY SUBMARINES

At its height, the United States Navy Polaris force consisted of over 40 submarines, of which roughly half would be on patrol at any one time. These formidable submarines weighed over 8,000 tons and carried 16 missiles, each with a range of 2,500 miles. The Royal Navy's Resolution Class submarines were very similar in size and shape. Their job at sea was to be in a position to respond instantly to any pre-emptive strike against a NATO country.

THE TOTEM POLE

The totem pole was the mascot of HMS *Totem*, a submarine from an earlier generation. It still stands as a continuing symbol of the submarine as a hunter. During the Cold War, Western SSNs monitored the whereabouts of Soviet nuclear submarines. They also acted as the first line of defence for Aircraft Carrier battle fleets and friendly SSBNs in the cat and mouse game of war beneath the sea.

CRUISE MISSILES

In the early 1990s another capability was added to *Los Angeles* class SSN's with the fitting of vertical launched Tomahawk cruise missiles. This inertial guided missile can be fired against land or ship targets out to ranges in excess of 2,000 kms. It is guided by a map in its memory against land targets, and flies at very low level. It came to prominence during the first Gulf War against Iraq when a reporter from CNN watched one fly past his hotel window!

BACK TO BASE

In addition to providing facilities for rest (a comfortable bed) and recreation (opportunities for sport) for crews when they return from patrol, the submarine's base also houses workshops and medical facilities. Between patrols, the men have an opportunity for men to spend time with their families, as well as repairing machinery to prepare the submarine for her next commitment. Refreshed and repaired, both man and machine will be ready once again for many weeks or months at sea.

SEAL DELIVERY VEHICLE

The modern equivalent for landing special forces such as the American SEALS is the United States Navy Mk VIII Delivery Vehicle. Like World War II, the 'Chariots' in the Swimmer Delivery Vehicle is carried by a mother submarine to the vicinity of the target objective. The great advantages of the combination are that the SEAL team is landed in total secrecy, and without them being exhausted by having to paddle for miles!

GIANT AIRCRAFT CARRIERS

After the Second World War the US Navy began building aircraft carriers much bigger than any previous warships. Today 13 are in service, each with a displacement of up to 102,000 tons. The flight deck is over 300 metres (1,000 ft) long, and there are over 40 mess decks (restaurants) for the 6,000 ship's crew and aircrew on board. Each evening those off duty have a choice of 25 cinemas. When in action the rapid launch and recovery of aircraft is almost like a ballet, with differently coloured deck crews each playing a choreographed role.

LANDING ON A CARRIER

This Boeing F-18 Hornet is about to hit the deck of a US Navy carrier. The pilot has lowered the landing gear and the long arrester hook at the tail, and put the wing in the high-lift configuration with the leading and trailing edges all hinged sharply downwards. Guided by electronic systems (in the old days pilots were guided by a batsman standing on deck with things like brightly coloured table-tennis bats) the pilot aims to hit the deck just beyond the first of several arrester wires stretched across the ship. The long hook should pick up one of these strong cables even before the wheels slam brutally on to the deck. The momentum of the aircraft pulls the wire out, resisted by a system of cable drums, stopping the aircraft sharply.

THE SEA VIXEN

This big de Havilland aircraft had powerful radar in the nose operated by a second crew-member in what was called 'the coal hole' low down on the right of the pilot. The armament was a mixture of four large guided missiles and various rockets or bombs. Vixens could dive faster than sound.

Naval Jets

From the earliest days of fighters, attempts had been made to operate them from warships. Naval planes had been launched from lighters (flat barges) towed behind fast destroyers. In the Second World War fighters operated from British, American and Japanese aircraft carriers. Most did not last long, because they tended to crash on returning to the ship.

But by the end of the War, in August 1945, aircraft designers knew how to make naval aircraft strong enough to stand up to the violent stresses of being shot off catapults, smashed down on heaving decks and then suddenly brought to a halt by arrester wires. There was also a need to have folding wings, so that they could be taken down in small lifts and tightly packed in hangars.

By the time peace returned jet fighters were taking over, with improved electronic navigation aids. In the 1950s a series of new ideas were introduced: the angled flight deck, the powerful steam catapult, and the mirror sight to help guide pilots on deck in bad weather.

UNFOLDING THE WINGS

This Grumman F9F of the US Navy's 'Blue Angels' aerobatic team is unfolding its wings before being catapulted off the deck of an aircraft carrier. Naval aircraft are designed to fold their wings so that more can be packed into congested hangars below deck. The F9F entered service soon after the Second World War, and saw service in the Korean War of 1950-3.

SIDEWINDER MISSILE

The Sidewinder was invented by the US Navy in 1953 as a guided missile able to home (steer itself) on to the heat radiated by a target aircraft. Originally weighing only just over 45 kg (100 lb), it was the simplest and cheapest guided missile in its class. The heat-seeking guidance was in the nose, steering the missile via the four pivoted nose fins. Next came the warheads, followed by the rocket motor. On the fixed tail fins were small flywheels which spun at high speed to give the weapon stability. They are named after a venomous snake which in the same way senses heat emitted by its victims.

Supersonic Fighters

LIGHTNING

The prototype of this outstanding British fighter first flew on 4 April 1957. On the same day the Government said fighters were obsolete and that the RAF did not need any! This crippled the development of the Lightning, and the RAF and British aircraft industry took years to recover. Uniquely, the Lightning had a wing swept back at 60 degrees and two Rolls-Royce Avon turbojets one above the other. The bulge underneath is an extra fuel tank, and the small projections on each side of the nose carried missiles (not fitted here). The Lightning could reach twice the speed of sound.

In 1945 documents captured from Germany showed that jets could be made to fly faster if their wings were 'swept' (angled back like an arrowhead). The first such fighter to fly (in 1948) was the North American F-86 Sabre. It was 161 km/h (100 mph) faster than 'straight-wing' jets and in a dive it could fly faster than sound. Residents of Los Angeles began hearing strange bangs, and it was soon realized that they were caused by the supersonic fighter's shockwaves reaching the ground. Designers began to fit more powerful engines so that fighters could fly faster than sound on the level. The Convair F-102, a radar-equipped interceptor with a delta (triangular) wing and fin, was supposed to be supersonic but proved too slow. In 1954 it was urgently redesigned according to new aerodynamic discoveries and it reached Mach 1.25 (1.25 times the speed of sound) with the original engine. By 1956 it was developed into the F-106, exceeding Mach 2 and setting a record at 2,454 km/h (1,525 mph). Many countries added to the sophistication of design, engine power, and aerodynamics of the supersonic fighter but no other aircraft yet has matched the Soviet MiG-31 and MiG-31M for their combined speed and range, their power, radar ability and enormous air-to-air missiles.

A DOUBLE DELTA

The Swedes called their Saab 35 Draken (Dragon) a double delta because it had a delta wing mounted on the ends of an inner wing of even more extreme delta shape. Thus, all the fuel tanks, electronics and other items were arranged from front to rear. Despite its amazing shape, the Draken prototype, flown in 1955, was very successful, and eventually Saab built 600 including a few for Denmark and Finland. Some were passed on from Sweden to the Austrian air force.

DELTA-WING FIGHTER

The F-102A had wings and vertical tail that were in a perfectly triangular shape (named 'delta' after the Greek letter). This shape enables the wing to be very thin yet stronger than wings of ordinary shape, and the short span (distance from tip to tip) makes it suitable for supersonic speeds. The penalty of small wings is the need for longer runways as such aircraft need to take off and land at high speeds.

'MISSILE WITH A MAN IN IT'

This is what Lockheed called their F-104 Starfighter when it was revealed in 1956. It was designed to meet the criticisms of US pilots who had fought in the Korean War and had been outflown by the MiG-15. It was designed to climb very steeply and fly faster than any enemy plane. Features included a single powerful engine, tiny razor-edged wings, a high tailplane and a pilot seat that ejected downwards.

'CHUCK' YEAGER

Major (later General) Charles E. Yeager was a fighter pilot in the United States Army Air Force (USAAF) during the Second World War. In peacetime he became a test pilot and flew the Bell XS-1 to become the first human to fly faster than the speed of sound on 14 October 1947.

STAR WARS

Both American and Russian satellite technology was based on the enormous advances in rocketry made by German scientists during World War II, when the V2 rocket was developed. The first communications satellite, 'Sputnik I', was successfully put into orbit by the Russians in 1957. Today, our skies are littered with several hundred communications satellites to aid the spread of information technology via computers, an essential part of modern missile warfare. The Strategic Defensive Initiative ('Star Wars') was a proposed system of orbiting space stations to detect and launch guided missiles.

AERIAL RECONNAISSANCE

One of the earliest uses to which both cameras and aeroplanes were put was to take aerial photographs of enemy positions. Developed during World War I, by the time of the Second World War a whole branch of the military secret service was engaged on interpreting the details of aerial photographs to follow troop movements and pinpoint bombing targets.

ELITE FORCE

Throughout history elite specialist forces have been employed to carry out specific missions, mostly in secret, and often used during peace-time when a government might not want to be linked to certain sensitive operations. Britain's Special Air Services (the SAS.) is generally regarded as one of the finest and most effective of these. Training is rigorous and only those capable of survival in the toughest conditions are selected.

THE US MARINES

Only the best and toughest troops are selected for the US Marine Corps. Personnel are trained in multi-skills, including air, sea and land tactics, and are capable of survival when dropped behind enemy lines. They are often the expeditionary force sent in to first engage an enemy and clear the way for the main military thrust to follow and as such usually face the fiercest opposition.

Special Forces & Espionage

Armies have always used spies to gain advance notice of an enemy's plans. Espionage was a particular feature of the 'Cold War' between the West and Russia, when both sides rearmed after World War II, and continues to flourish in today's world of sophisticated information technology. One of the most effective methods of secret warfare is for a small group of patriotic individuals to adopt guerrilla tactics against an enemy. The Boers used it against Britain in 1899-1902 and the Japanese during World War II. Its most effective employment in modern times, however, was probably by the North Vietnamese against the Americans, who were forced to adopt a strategy of defoliating the jungle to remove the guerrillas' cover.

ATTACK BY REMOTE CONTROL

A whole range of cruise missiles now exists, including the nuclear-armed Tomahawk, which can be launched from the ground, or from aircraft, submarines or warships, and directed by sophisticated computers to their targets. The Patriot missile (shown left) is a highly advanced mobile battlefield SAM (Surface-to-Air-Missile) system. It uses phased array radar for accurate target detection at several hundred kilometres and employs anti-jamming devices.

GUERRILLA WARFARE

When faced with the superior forces of a more powerful enemy, the smaller military forces of a patriotic or revolutionary movement often resort to guerrilla tactics. By dividing and isolating the enemy and making lightning strikes when least expected, such fighters can often create stalemate situations or even defeat a superior enemy. Guerrilla movements also usually have the added advantage of being able to mobilise the local population against the common enemy and being able to conceal themselves amongst them. From such a vantage point they can strike right at the heart of an enemy with sudden acts of harassment or terrorism.

EARLY WARNING SYSTEMS

The first advance warning system to detect approaching aircraft was Radar (Radio Detection And Ranging). It was invented in 1935 by Robert Watson-Watt and worked by transmitting radio waves and then scanning the returning echoes to measure the distance and position of the reflecting object. It was fitted to the Boeing B-17 'Flying Fortress' bomber, making it the first 'self defending' aeroplane. The system has been greatly advanced since then. The jet shown here has been specially adapted to carry an AWACS system (Airborne Warning And Control System). It carries long-range surveillance and detection radar with C3 (Command, Communication and Control) facilities to detect friendly aircraft, in addition to several other sophisticated tracking devices.

SHIPS' STORES

The modern fleet, often at sea for months at a time, relies on its fleet train of auxiliary ships to provide the backup of stores, fuel and ammunition. Modern supply ships like the British Royal Fleet Auxiliary Service's *Fort Grange* Class provide the front-line ships with everything they need. Able to carry troops and helicopters, they can also support amphibious (on-land) operations. For self-defence they are armed with a few light anti-aircraft guns.

MARINES

Major warships carry a detachment of elite troops trained in all aspects of raiding and commando warfare. They can be put into trouble spots by their ship's helicopter or, as here, by fast rigid inflatable craft. Whichever nation they belong to, these 'sea soldiers' are fiercely proud of the traditions of their corps.

GUIDED MISSILES

This harpoon would not be found in a whaling ship! The Macdonnell Douglas Harpoon missile is radar-guided and accurate to 70 nautical miles. Almost as fast as Concorde, this powerful anti-ship weapon carries a 227kg warhead. The slower Tomahawk SLCM (ship-launched cruise missile) can carry a nuclear or conventional warhead to a land target at a range of 700 nautical miles.

SHIP'S BRAIN

Ships in battle were once controlled from the quarterdeck or the bridge, but the Combat Information Centre (CIC) is the 'brain' of the modern warship. Sophisticated radar and sonar equipment can detect any threat and computer guided weapons and countermeasure devices will deal with it. Pinpoint satellite navigation systems and communications links bring an accuracy that admirals of the past could only dream of. The men and women of modern navies have to keep up with all this technology and are constantly mastering new techniques.

Warships Today

The demands on modern navies are as varied now as at any time in the past. With the Cold War long behind us, the emphasis is on peacekeeping rather than war. Today's warships are used to police international security agreements. The importance of air superiority to many of these tasks ensures that aircraft carriers and carrier groups remain central to naval plans. But new technologies, and the race to stay ahead of the threats that they pose to warships, are already changing the shapes and capabilities of the next generation of cruisers and destroyers. As with every development in ship design over the centuries, these changes are affecting not only tactical and strategic matters, but the way every ship is commanded, and even the demands upon each member of the crew.

ARMS CACHE

Where once cruisers had menacing gun turrets, this US Navy *Ticonderoga* Class cruiser has apparently plain areas of deck. But, hidden beneath the hatches, there are over 120 land-attack, anti-ship and surface-to-air guided missiles at the ready, all precision-controlled by the ship's sophisticated technical systems. Just in case, these cruisers also carry automatic 5-inch guns, torpedoes and rapid firing anti-missile defences.

USS *ARLEIGH BURKE*

First of her class of 28 ships, this 1991-built destroyer has the rakish look of those of the past but capabilities none of them could match. Equipped with the Aegis system, she is designed for an air defence role, and armed with missiles, guns and powerful electronic countermeasures. Ten future ships of this class will carry a helicopter, adding to an already impressive range of abilities.

Ships of the Future

PROJECT HORIZON

As warships become ever more expensive to design and build, seafaring nations are pooling their resources. In Project Horizon, the British, German and Italian navies are producing the next generation of surface warships. Note the uncluttered sloping super-structure: with no hard edges, this ship will give very little radar echo.

The warships of the future may look very different to the current generation of vessels. 'Stealth' technology will give rise to strange angular shapes, which minimise a ship's radar signature. Hull forms such as catamarans and trimarans may be adopted, new materials will become available, 'smart' weapons will be replaced by 'brilliant' ones and advanced propulsion systems will make ships and submarines quieter and ever harder to detect electronically. But of course, there will be advances in the means of detection at the same time. With new technologies will come new ships and new seamanship. Only the ancient hazards of the sea will remain the same.

THE SHAPE OF THINGS TO COME

A design proposal from the innovative warship builders Thornycroft, the *Sea Wraith* corvette explores the angular sculptural forms of stealth technology. To some eyes, her long, low proportions and the backward raking bow hark back 2,500 years to the Athenian trireme.

ELECTRONIC CAMOUFLAGE

In service since 1996, *La Fayette* has many of the features that will soon become familiar. Angled surfaces disperse the signal from incoming radar, while amazing new materials and paints absorb much of the rest. This frigate will be with the French fleet for many years to come.

FLOATING LABORATORY

The *Sea Shadow* has been in service since the early 1980s. On this floating test-bed, the US Navy experiments with new materials, equipment and techniques. The lessons learnt here will affect the development of warships in the 21st century.

THE GREAT SUBMARINE RACE

The two biggest navies in the world belong to the United States and Russia who have the greatest numbers of submarines. Other nations that operate nuclear powered submarines, and possess ballistic missiles, are China, Britain and France. Many more countries operate diesel-electric submarines, with new entries into the market being Iran, and in the near future, Malaysia.

MODERN CONDITIONS

Whatever the nationality, life at sea in a submarine is not comfortable, but at least today it is tolerable. The two sailors in their bunks show how crowded living spaces are, and how necessary it is for the submariner to get on with his fellow-man! The bunk is the only 'private' space available, demonstrated by the young sailor writing a letter home.

UP TO DATE MACHINES

The modern diesel electric submarine can vary in size from almost 3000 tons down to 450 tons. The submarine pictured belongs to the Japanese Maritime Defence Force, which operates about 16 of them in two flotillas at Kure and Yokosuka. They are highly capable, being fitted with the latest in sonar technology, and armed with long range torpedoes and Sub-Harpoon radar homing anti-ship missiles. They carry 20 weapons and have a top speed of 20 knots when submerged. They are manned by a crew of 75.

ENDURANCE AT SEA

One of the great demands on the submarine is that it remains at sea for long periods, often far from base. It is essential therefore that it can take care of itself so that it does not have to keep rushing back to harbour for repairs. For example, the diving team on board can fix irritating external rattles!

INTERIOR DESIGNS

The interior of this French nuclear powered ballistic missile submarine shows how big they have become! There are now three decks to negotiate, with masses of machinery as far as the eye can see. Crew size is about 120 men. The French submarine force is a powerful one with 6 SSBNs, 6 SSNs, and 7 diesel electric submarines. Their attack submarines (SSNs) have a speed of 25 knots.

SEA MONSTERS

The Russian *Typhoon* SSBN, weighing 26,000 tons when submerged, is the largest submarine ever built. It is 562 feet (171 metres) long, and carries 20 ballistic missiles, each with 6-9 warheads each. In addition to her *Typhoons*, Russia has *Delta* Class SSBNs, and is expected to maintain an operational force of about 25 of them. She also has about 50 SSNs, some with anti-land cruise missile capability, and 40 diesel electric submarines.

Modern Submarines

Politically and economically the world is an ever changing place. Since the fall of the Berlin Wall there have been a number of treaty realignments in Europe. In addition, particularly in the Far East and South America, we have seen the emergence of what were formerly 'developing' countries as powerful economies. What remains unchanged is the total reliance on the sea by maritime nations for the transport of their export merchandise and import of essential raw materials. Indeed since 1950, because of the growth of container traffic, seaborne trade has increased twelve fold. For maritime nations the interruption of this trade could threaten their economic survival. So it is vital for world stability that international shipping routes are kept free and open, and this can only be achieved by the protection of well trained naval forces. Submarines in the hands of an aggressor could be used with devastating effect against harbours and merchant shipping. Many countries, conscious of the lessons of history, are now adding submarines to their navies as a deterrent to potential foes.

DEEP SEA EXPLORATION

The oil industry has benefited hugely from the ability of submarines to lay and inspect pipelines - potentially avoiding major pollution threats to the oceans. Submarines have also helped scientists to explore the deepest parts of the world's oceans, photographing and investigating shipwrecks such as that of the *Titanic*.

Today's Fighters

It is remarkable that the history of the fighter plane has seen just 30 years of piston-engined fighters (1915-45) and over 60 years of jets. In this time fighters have become bigger and heavier, far more powerful, incredibly more complicated and much more expensive. An unexpected development in today's fighters is that instead of the fighter getting faster, it has almost gone in reverse. In 1954 the first supersonic fighters reached over Mach 1 and went on to reach Mach 2. The MiG-25 nudged Mach 3. At such a speed aircraft must travel in almost straight lines. To manoeuvre, that speed must be brought right down. The French Dassault Mirage family all reached Mach 2.2, but their latest fighter, the Rafale, cannot exceed Mach 1.8. Some of the greatest of today's fighters are products of the former Soviet design teams, such as MiG and Sukhoi. Both have twin engines hung under a very efficient wing which, merged into the body and with powerful horizontal tails and twin fins, gives it outstanding manoeuvrability.

THE GREATEST?

One of the largest modern fighters is the Sukhoi Su-27, designed in Moscow and produced by a factory in Komsomolsk-na-Amur in far Siberia. It could be clumsy and unimpressive, but in fact many experts consider it the most formidable in the sky. Powered by two AL-31 engines, it has tremendous performance, and such test pilots as Evgenii Frolov have demonstrated manoeuvres – such as the upward-tilt 'Cobra' – that no Western fighter can copy. Su-27s and various successors carry a spectrum of missiles far superior to anything currently available in the West.

A COBRA MANOEUVRE

This manoeuvre was first performed in 1989 by Sukhoi test pilot Viktor Pugachev. He astonished the world by rotating his aircraft, nose up, through 120 degrees and then back to horizontal, with the flight path remaining horizontal.

PRODUCTION LINE

In 1972 the USAF invited manufacturers to submit ideas for a 'light fighter', much cheaper than the massive F-15 Eagle then in production. There was no suggestion the winner would actually be put into production, far less adopted by the United States Air Force (USAF), but before long the General Dynamics F-16 Fighting Falcon had gained so many customers it had far surpassed the F-15. Today a product of Lockheed Martin, later versions of F-16 are still in production at this factory at Fort Worth, Texas.

COST OF MODERN FIGHTERS

In the Second World War a Spitfire cost about £6,000, but today a single F-22 (left) costs over £60 million. Thus, for the price of one modern fighter, one could in theory have bought 10,000 Spitfires.

FIGHTER ENGINE

Today all fighters have turbofan engines, in which the air coming in at the inlet is divided. Some is compressed and then goes through the combustion chamber and turbines, while the rest is bypassed and mixed with the hot gas at the back. This Russian AL-31FP is one of a pair fitted to the Su-27. It has a maximum thrust of 13,300 kg (29,320 lb), and a special feature is that its jet nozzle can be vectored (swivelled) to exert powerful control on the aircraft. On top are all the fuel controls, starter, electric generator, hydraulic pumps and other accessories.

SEA HARRIER

In the Falklands War in 1982 the British Aerospace Harrier of the RAF and Sea Harrier of the Royal Navy enabled the Argentine invaders to be defeated. Without these quite small aircraft it would have been impossible even to consider retaking the islands. No other aircraft can rule the skies and also attack ground targets without needing an airfield. This is because of the development of jet nozzles which can be directed downwards so the aircraft can take off and land vertically.

RAFALE

France's next-generation fighter is the Rafale (French for 'squall'). Made by the Dassault company, which since 1955 has delivered thousands of Mirage fighters, the Rafale has two engines and a controllable foreplane just above and ahead of the delta wing. Different versions are being produced for the Armée de l'Air (air force) and Aéronavale (navy). This Rafale has a clumsy fixed probe on the nose for taking on fuel in flight; most flight-refuelling probes are retractable.

A EUROFIGHTER COCKPIT

Best of the future European fighters is the Eurofighter, made by Britain, Germany, Italy and Spain in collaboration. Here, beyond the advanced ejection seat, can be seen the control column and then the instrument panel dominated by big multifunction displays. As far as possible these displays are blank, showing the pilot only what he needs to know. Should anything go wrong he can push buttons to find out as much detail as he wishes. In the centre of the windscreen is the optically flat glass of the computerized gunsight.

F-22 RAPTOR

This strange name, meaning a bird of prey, has been chosen for the most important fighter in production today, being produced by Lockheed Martin for the USAF. It is a very large aircraft, yet because it is specially designed for what is called 'stealth' it is almost invisible on enemy radars. It has a huge wing and large tailplanes, and all the missiles are carried internally. Beside the fuselage are the big lozenge (diamond) shaped air inlets for the jet engines.

Fighter Planes

ntil the jet era, new fighters could be designed, developed and put into production in a few weeks. Today, despite the availability of computers that can slash the time needed for complex calculations, the same tasks can take anything up to 10 years. Thus, the Eurofighter was a detailed feasibility study in 1984, but did not enter service until after 2002. Co-operation between the four collaborating countries was slow but eventually the Eurofighter flew in March 1994. However, when test flying began, it had long been obvious that future fighters should have vectoring nozzles, able to swivel so the plane could thrust in different directions. Such nozzles may be available at the Eurofighter's mid-life update in 2007. Shape is also central to the performance of future fighters – to reduce the size of the reflection on enemy radar screens. The Lockheed Martin F-22 Raptor has two very powerful engines whose nozzles can not only vector but also discharge the jets through flat slits. This is all part of the trend towards 'stealth' design, which makes them hardly detectable on enemy radar. After the F-22, the next generation is the JSF (Joint Strike Fighter), a US multi-service programme in which Britain has a small share. Some designs have powerful engines with the VTOL (vertical takeoff and landing) capability of the Harrier.

AIR SHOW

Around the world millions of people like to go to air shows. Some of these, such as Farnborough in England and Paris in France, are trade shows where new aircraft are demonstrated to possible customers. Others are purely for fun, where crowds are thrilled by formation aerobatic teams such as the RAF's Red Arrows (as shown here).

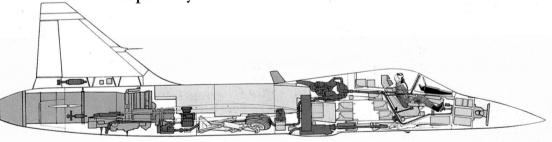

GRIPEN

Probably the smallest fighter in production in the world is Sweden's Saab Gripen (Griffin). Its engine is similar to that of the Hornet, but it carries only one engine instead of two. Like the Rafale, the Gripen has a foreplane and a delta wing, a gun in the fuselage and missiles under the wing and on the wingtips.

Today's Pilots

The enormous increase in military flying in the Second World War led to rapid technical advances of all kinds, though many did not come into use until the conflict was over. Several of these developments affected pilots' clothing. In a steep turn, with the wings banked to an angle of 60 degrees, the acceleration is 2g (twice gravity), so your weight appears to have doubled. Planes at the end of the Second World War could reach about 6g, so the pilot had to keep a tight hold of the stick (control column) to stop his arm being wrenched off downwards. A sustained 6g turn will make most people 'black out'; they remain conscious but their eyes go dark and they can no longer see. Vision is restored on recovery to straight and level flight. To help counter this and other problems of violent manoeuvres, a special kind of flying clothing was developed.

MODERN PILOT

Comfortable in a Mk 14 ejection seat, this fighter pilot is all kitted up ready for action. Modern fighter seats are very complex and cost many times more than a complete Second World War fighter.

COMBAT SIMULATOR

Whereas flight simulators help pilots to learn to master their aircraft, a combat simulator trains him to dogfight with enemy aircraft. It is inside a giant dome, on the inside of which the pilot sees the ground, the sky and other aircraft. Today there are so many computer games that there are thousands of potential fighter pilots!

FIGHTER COCKPIT

This is the cockpit of an F-16 Fighting Falcon simulator. In the distance can be seen 'enemies'. The pilot gets all the information he needs from the large square displays in front of him, each like a clever reprogrammable TV. Some guide his flight and help him find enemies, while others tell him about his own aircraft. Whereas other fighters have a traditional big control column ('joystick'), the F-16 pilot flies holding a small grip shaped to fit his hand on the right edge of the cockpit.

BONEDOME HELMET

Today fighter pilots wear a strong but light helmet which protects their heads if they should be violently bumped against the cockpit canopy. In combat, pilots were sometimes knocked out when they wore floppy leather helmets.

LIMB GARTERS

Both the pilot's legs are encircled by strong straps, one above the knee and the other round the calf. On ejection, the legs are pulled in and the pilot's arms are also restrained to avoid hitting the cockpit or being injured by windblast.

BOOTS

Fighter pilots wear strong boots with long laces. These help him push hard on the rudder or wheel brake pedals and protect him if he has to eject.

'TOP GUN'

This Hollywood blockbuster starring Tom Cruise as a maverick US fighter pilot also stars two of today's top fighter planes – the Grumman F-14 Tomcat carrier-based fighter of the US Navy, and the Soviet MiG.

FIRING HANDLE

Between the pilot's thighs is the black and yellow striped firing handle. This triggers a complicated computer-controlled sequence on which his life depends.

THE FLYING SUIT

Even today the standard attire of a fighter pilot is the overall. This Japanese pilot is not ready to fly. His cap would be replaced by the complex 'bonedome' helmet with oxygen mask, communications and other services.

EJECTION!

After the Second World War it was found that jet aircraft could fly so fast that, in an emergency, the pilot could not just 'bale out'. To escape by parachute he had to be shot out. Gradually ejection seats were made safer (early types sometimes painfully damaged the spine) and today the Martin-Baker Mk 14 is typical of the refined types on offer. Modern seats are shot out by a propulsion system incorporating a rocket, which can be seen firing here. A small chute is deployed to slow the seat down. Finally the pilot is released from the seat as his own parachute deploys automatically.

GLOSSARY

aft Near the rear of a ship or plane.

artillery Missile-launching weapons. In ancient times, these were bows and catapults, later cannons, and today artillery refers to modern missile launchers.

ballista An ancient weapon like a huge crossbow, used for shooting large missiles.

ballistic missile A missile guided to the top of its arch and then free-falling.

bilges The lowest part of a ship's inner hull.

biplane A plane with two pairs of wings.

boom A spar at the bottom of a mast, used to hold the foot of a sail.

bow The front of a ship.

breech-loading A gun designed to be loaded at the rear.

broadside 1. All of the guns on one side of the ship. 2. To fire all of these guns at once.

bulkhead A partition, dividing a ship into compartments, to prevent the spread of fire or water.

calibre The diameter of a bullet, the inside of a gun or an artillery shell.

canopy The large fabric part of a parachute that opens to catch the air.

capstan A device for lifting heavy weights, consisting of a vertical cylinder, around which a cable is wound.

carrack A large sailing ship used in the 15th, and 16th centuries.

cog A small sailing ship with one mast.

conning tower An observation post on the top of a submarine, used for navigation.

convoy A group of ships travelling together for safety, sometimes with a protective escort

cruise missile A low-flying guided missile.

empire One country ruling over several other countries.

feudal system A system of government where vassals worked for a lord in return for protection.

first-rate A category for British navy ships in the 17th and 18th century. First-rate ships were large with 100 guns or more, usually arranged in three decks. Second-rate ships had about 90 guns, arranged in three decks. Third-rate ships had about 70 guns, arranged in two decks. All three categories were ships of the line.

frescoes A type of painting where colour is applied to fresh plaster.

frigate A medium sized warship.

fuselage The central part of an aircraft, where the crew, passengers and cargo are carried.

galleon A large sailing ship with three masts, usually Spanish.

galley A large ship, usually propelled by oars.

Great Ship Battleship of the British navy during the 15th, 16th and 17th centuries.

guerrilla A member of an independent military unit which carries out surprise raids and sabotage.

GLOSSARY

hull The frame of a ship.

infantry Soldiers trained to fight on foot.

jet Part of an engine that provides the lifting power for an aircraft.

ketch A type of ship with two masts.

knot One nautical mile (1.85km/1.15 miles) per hour.

line of battle A tactic of naval warfare where a fleet of ships form a line to attack. The advantage is that they can all fire a broadside without hitting each other. See also the glossary entry for ship of the line and first-rate.

Mach Measurement which relates the speed of an aircraft to the speed of sound. Mach 1 is the speed of sound (1,225 kmh/765 mph) Mach 2 is twice the speed of sound.

mizzen mast The third mast.

monoplane A plane with one pair of wings.

mortar A cannon used to fire a missile in a high trajectory.

palisade A strong fence made of wooden poles.

poop A raised deck on the stern (back) of the ship.

propeller A machine with spinning blades that provides thrust to lift an aircraft.

ram A heavy beam used by attackers to batter their way into a castle or a ship.

rig The arrangement of masts and sails on a ship.

scorched earth Destroying farms and other land as a tactic in war.

ship of the line A large, powerful warship, built to be used in a line of other ships during battle. See also the glossary entry for line of battle and first-rate.

sloop A type of sailing ship with one mast.

sonar A system using sound waves to locate objects underwater.

SSBN A United State's navy classification, describing a nuclear submarine with ballistic missile capability.

SSN A United State's navy classification, describing a nuclear submarine.

stealth Technology used to make a ship or plane almost invisible to radar.

stern The rear part of a ship or plane.

stressed-skin The outer covering of a plane, designed to cope with the stresses and forces encountered in flight.

supersonic Faster than the speed of sound.

tail The rear part of the fuselage that balances a plane.

torpedo An underwater missile.

trireme An ancient warship that had three rows of oars on each side.

turbo System that increases a vehicle's power by forcing more air into the engine.

wolf pack A tactic where a group of submarines attacked a convoy of ships.

INDEX

INDEX

INDEX